THE SUPREME COURT

AND

THE CONSTITUTION

THE SUPREME COURT
AND
THE CONSTITUTION

CHARLES A. BEARD

Introduction and Bibliographies by
ALAN F. WESTIN

DOVER PUBLICATIONS, INC.
Mineola, New York

Bibliographical Note

This Dover edition, first published in 2006, is a republication of the work originally published in the Classics in History Series by Prentice-Hall, Inc., Englewood Cliffs, N.J., in 1962. The 1962 edition, in turn, was a republication, with an introduction and bibliographies by Alan F. Westin, of the work first published by The Macmillan Company, New York, in 1912. The original Editors' Note and the two biographical paragraphs printed at the beginning of the 1962 edition have been omitted in the present volume.

Library of Congress Cataloging-in-Publication Data

Beard, Charles Austin, 1874–1948.
   The Supreme Court and the constitution / Charles A. Beard ; introduction and bibliographies by Alan F. Westin. — Dover ed.
     p. cm.
   Originally published: Englewood Cliffs, N.J. : Prentice-Hall, 1962, in series: Classics in history series.
   Includes bibliographies.
   ISBN 0-486-44779-0 (pbk.)
   1. United States. Supreme Court. 2. Judicial review—United States. 3. Constitutional history—United States. I. Title.

KF4575.B39 2006
347.73'26—dc22

                                                2005054771

Manufactured in the United States of America
Dover Publications, Inc., 31 East 2nd Street, Mineola, N.Y. 11501

Table of Contents

Introduction

Charles Beard and American Debate
Over Judicial Review, 1790-1961

Seventeen decades and fourteen Chief Justices after the adoption of the Federal Constitution, why should anyone still debate whether the Framers intended the Supreme Court to pass on the constitutionality of Congressional legislation? In terms of parsing the records of the Convention and the text of the Constitution itself, putting these into the context of colonial and republican America, and collecting the memoirs and correspondence of the day —surely, the job has been done by now and the issue must be considered settled by all except the hopelessly antiquarian.

Such was the view taken, for example, by Professor Felix Frankfurter as long ago as 1924. Dismayed by public charges that the Supreme Court had "usurped" the power of judicial review, Frankfurter attributed the "persistence of this talk" to a "lack of historical scholarship, combined with fierce prepossessions. . . . One would suppose that, at least, after the publication of Beard, *The Supreme Court and the Constitution,* there would be an end to this empty controversy." [1]

Charles Beard shared this view of his 1912 study. In the introduction to a re-issue of the work in 1938, he announced firmly:

For practical purposes, [my] book settled the controversy. . . . The ghost of usurpation was fairly laid. Whatever controversies may arise in the future over the exercise of judicial power, it is not

---

[1] Felix Frankfurter, "A Note on Advisory Opinions," 37 *Harv. L. Rev.* 1002 (1924), p. 1003.

likely that the historic right of the Supreme Court to pass upon acts of Congress will aga:n be seriously challenged.

Despite Beard's prophecy, the "ghost of usurpation" has been clanking its chains through legislative chambers, historical meetings, and publishing houses for many a decade since 1912. Several dozen books and perhaps a hundred articles have persisted in treating this as still a debatable proposition, and not all of the commentators can be dismissed as incompetents or outraged partisans deprived of reason.

To probe the reasons for this continuing debate and to assess the relation of Beard's study to it, this introductory essay has been divided into four sections. Part I summarizes, in brief fashion, the classic lines of debate over the Supreme Court's power to review acts of Congress. Part II examines critically the sources of conflict and debate over this judicial authority. Part III surveys the literature on the Framers' intention as to judicial review of Congressional measures and analyzes certain major periods into which this literature falls. Part IV presents the basic criticisms which have been leveled against the Beard thesis. In a final coda, the essay suggests why the debate over judicial review will never be settled, and why this continued argument should be a source of satisfaction rather than one of concern for a free society.

I. The Classic Lines of Debate Over
Judicial Review of Legislation

Before exploring why the debate over judicial review of legislation has continued with such vitality, it is useful to set out the classic assumptions and disputed positions in the controversy. The goal at this point is not to analyze these but only to catalogue them for future reference in this essay.

The pivot on which the entire debate revolves is that the Framers did not state, unequivocally and in a way which would foreclose the argument for all reasonable men reading the Constitution, that the

Supreme Court had the power to review Congressional measures and hold them invalid if the Justices thought them unconstitutional.[2] The situation resembles those of the President's inherent powers to act as chief executive or the Congress' power to spend for the general welfare. In all three, the Framers created an appearance of authority and a description of it in vague terms, but did not draft with sufficient precision to resolve serious ambiguities. Time and the development of our political system have made these provisions central to American constitutional debate, but the Framers spoke only once on these subjects and no constitutional amendments have been passed dealing with judicial review, inherent presidential powers, or spending for the general welfare. The result is that the debate has proceeded at the level of "original intention."

Coupled with this fact is the absence of comprehensive records of the Constitutional Convention to rely on for indications of intention. No transcript was taken at Philadelphia. We have the continuous notes of only one participant, James Madison, and meager, scattered notes from a few others. It is not too much to say that Madison's notes have become almost as disputed a written record as the text of the Constitution itself. Since the proceedings were secret, there is no newspaper coverage of the Convention, as there is for leading Congressional debates of the young Republic.

When the language of the Constitution is disputed, as here, there is a variety of criteria which can be used by the courts and by those speaking and writing about the issue as part of our constitutional politics. At least five such approaches can be identified. First, there is strict textual or word analysis, taking what the legislators put down on paper, defining it in dictionary fashion, and refusing to go beyond the words. The assumption of the textual school is that courts and executives should not re-write the Constitution; where ambiguities arise, the means of resolving them is constitutional amendment. A second approach is contextual analysis. Here,

---

[2] A copy of the Constitution, without the Amendments, has been printed in the Appendix and can be consulted for the references used in this Essay and in Beard's text.

the analyst considers not only the text but also the section of the Constitution in which it appears, as well as the document as a whole, to map the environments of meaning in which the Framers placed the disputed clauses. Strictly textual construction, say the contextualists, robs words of their roots in the interacting scheme of government which the Framers assembled to write and which the nation ratified. A third technique adds the drafting process to the net of analysis. Here the analyst studies the progress of the clause from its earliest Convention draft (and even its history as an idea or in other laws or jurisdictions before it reached the Convention), through committees and general debate, through amendments and final stylistic changes, to the final language. Words, in the view of the drafting process analysts, mean more when one examines what fell by the wayside, what was deliberately rejected, and what was heartily approved. A fourth technique might be called develop-mental analysis. It adds to the others a consideration of the accre-tions of meaning which the disputed clause has acquired from the time of its enactment to the time of analysis, based upon govern-mental practices involving the power in question, court interpre-tations, and changed economic and political conditions. The argu-ment for adding developmental factors is that, as the years advance since the original writing, increasingly broad constructions are needed to keep the purposes of the Framers in tune with new reali-ties. Finally, there is a fifth standard, one which is rarely supported openly but is as real as rock nevertheless. I would call this institu-tional analysis. In the case of the Supreme Court, as guardian of constitutional construction (including construction of its own pow-ers), this technique has the Justices manipulating the four above criteria in light of the values of society (as the Justices see them), particularly the values of consistency, predictability, and the pri-macy of the judiciary. Not all Justices would attach this institu-tional perspective, but a majority of the Court since Marshall's day has usually done so.

In the debate over judicial review of legislation, attention has centered on what I have called the drafting process phase of construction, usually termed, loosely, "the Framers' intent." Using a variety of points at which to measure intention—the selection process for members of the Convention, the Convention, the selection process for members of the Ratifying Convention, the Ratifying Conventions, public debate over ratification, contemporary events indicating the views on judicial power of members of the Convention or Ratifying Conventions, contemporary court practice, and various others—commentators have evolved four conflicting positions as to what the Framers intended when they defined judicial power. Again, to summarize:

(1) The Framers consciously provided for judicial review of Congressional acts, by writing express words to that effect into the text of the Constitution.

(2) The Framers consciously assumed this power would flow by normal implication from other powers given to the Court as well as from the logic of a written Constitution for a government of limited powers.

(3) The Framers were undecided whether to provide judicial review of legislation. The Convention ended without a conscious resolution of the issue and the Framers departed carrying divided assumptions as to whether judicial review would develop or not.

(4) The Framers considered the question of judicial review and deliberately left it out of the Constitution, because a majority was not convinced of its wisdom or necessity.

Over the decades, positions (2) and (3) have been the main battlefields, although (1) and (4) have had supporters from time to time.

To complete this catalogue of classic positions in the debate, we can summarize the items of evidence advanced to confirm or deny the legitimacy of this judicial power. Perhaps the best way to do this is to quote from one widely used summary of the arguments for and against. This summary, which follows on pages 6 and 7, is from a work[3] by Professor Percy Fenn, formerly of Oberlin, and has the merit of simplicity, if not of detail.

[3] Percy T. Fenn, *The Development of the Constitution* (New York: Appleton-Century-Crofts, Inc., 1948), pp. 10-12.

Arguments in favor of judicial review:

(1) The subordination of acts of Parliament to a higher law was known to English jurisprudence, because Sir Edward Coke said in Dr. Bonham's Case in 1610 that an act of Parliament contrary to the common law was void, or, at least, sometimes void.

(2) The Privy Council had the power to review judicially the acts of colonial legislatures and to annul them.

(3) James Otis, counsel in Paxton's Case in 1761, invoked a higher law—either divine law or the law of nature—to argue that it voided a legislative act made contrary to it.

(4) Eight precedents are alleged for the exercise of this power by state courts against state legislatures before 1787.

(5) The leading members of the Constitutional Convention knew of this power, advocated the grant of it, and thought they had granted it.

(6) Between 1789 and 1803 (the date of the federal Supreme Court's first use of it against Congress), ten state courts exerted this power against their legislatures.

(7) During this period, certain members of the Supreme Court claimed the power for the federal judiciary and used it on circuit.

Arguments against judicial review:

(1) Coke's dictum in the Bonham Case is contradicted by the whole theory and practice of parliamentary sovereignty.

(2) The Privy Council's power of review is of slight importance because (a) its position in relationship to a colonial legislature had no similarity either in fact or law to the position of a judiciary fixed as the third coordinate branch of an independent government; and because, further, (b) there is no record of the annulment of an important colonial law, if, indeed, it can be properly said that the Privy Council ever vetoed such a law.

(3) There is not one example of a colonial court exercising this power against an act of a colonial legislature.

(4) The alleged precedents for the exertion of this power by state courts are in most cases either unreliable or irrelevant for these reasons:

    (a) For one "case" there is no record at all.

    (b) For two of them, the opinions were written years after the case was decided, and by a friend of the court.

    (c) Several are of doubtful authenticity (the number varies with the writer).

(d) In most of them, the words claiming the power are mere dicta—the personal opinion of the judge, and not a ruling of the court—because the issue of constitutionality was not necessary for a decision of the controversy.

(5) The members of the Constitutional Convention never directly raised the question of the grant of such a power to the judiciary.

(6) The cases between 1787 and 1803 in which an act was voided did not occur before 1787.

(7) Chief Justice Marshall does not cite a single precedent for annulling a legislative act in *Marbury v. Madison*, which shows that he either did not know of any or did not think any important.

(8) Strong popular disapproval habitually attended the claim to exercise the judicial veto.

Which of these two sets of factual assertions and constitutional conclusions is the sounder raises, of course, the question of Beard's book, and of platoons of commentators long before and steadily after him.

Having set out the classic lines of the debate, we can now turn to several aspects in depth, particularly as they bear on Beard's thesis.

II. The Sources of Conflict Over "Judicial Usurpation"

There are a number of obvious reasons why attacks on the legitimacy of judicial review of federal legislation have been a permanent part of our constitutional discourse. Groups wounded by Supreme Court decisions, when the "provocation" is sustained and painful enough, will challenge the Court's authority as part of the disappointed group's arsenal of retaliation. Historians, legal commentators, and political scientists will sometimes join the attack as part of the policy-orientation of these persons; others will see the question of judicial review as a superb mystery to unravel for the sake of the problem itself. There are some other reasons, however, which are not quite as obvious and deserve some examination.

The particular manner in which the Supreme Court itself has treated the question of its power may be a prime explanation. In 1803, when John Marshall first announced for a unanimous bench in *Marbury v. Madison*[4] that the Court would hold a provision of federal law unconstitutional, he rested his argument on the principle of a written constitution, the nature of our governmental system, and the sworn obligation of federal Justices to apply the Constitution. There was no discussion of colonial practices, pre-Convention precedents, Convention debates, ratification proceedings, Congressional construction down to 1803, or any other supports from contemporary events. The opinion was a shimmering exercise in constitutional logic. And with this, Marshall launched judicial review on a choppy sea. Professor Charles Black, Jr., of Yale Law School has described well one aspect of this launching.

Marshall, intellectually, was one of those frightening people who have the air of seizing something by force even when picking up a plum of the ripest and readiest to fall. If Marshall had made it clear that he was using arguments put forward long before in *The Federalist,* to confirm and officially establish what was a pretty general understanding already stated by the Supreme Court, and if he had shown that he conceived his task not as that of demonstrating beyond the palest shadow of a doubt the correctness of the doctrine of judicial review, but rather as that of establishing that this doctrine had decidedly better claims than its contradictory, then perhaps the "usurpation" myth would have enjoyed less perennial appeal.[5]

Another sophisticated commentator has doubted whether an opinion such as Professor Black suggests would have served Marshall better, or even as well, as the one he wrote. Professor Robert McCloskey of Harvard has noted that Marshall chose to address his argument to those "who would deny the power of judicial review *altogether,*" those, in other words, who saw the constitutional sovereignty of Congress well fastened to the national tree and not at all ready to drop into the waiting basket of the judiciary. Marshall devoted his presentation to showing that a law which clearly

---

[4] 1 Cranch 137 (1803).
[5] Charles L. Black, Jr., *The People and the Court* (New York: The Macmillan Co., 1960), p. 26.

violated the Constitution, such as a duty on state exports in violation of Article I, section 9, would surely be something which the judges should not enforce.

Now many, though not all, of Marshall's listeners would probably concede this point as far as it goes; the real questions for them would arise when the statute was not a *clear* violation of the Consitution, or when judges purported to speak on constitutional questions not only for themselves but for the other branches as well, to presume that the judicial finding of invalidity was final. These queries are not met at all in the argument of the *Marbury* case, and by ignoring them Marshall succeeds in beclouding them. Attacks on the discretionary scope and the finality of judicial review are henceforth confused with attacks on the minimal power Marshall here contends for, and the attackers thus find that though they aim for the weakest point in the judicial armor they almost invariably hit the strongest. The *Marbury* argument is justly celebrated, but not the least of its virtues is the fact that it is somewhat beside the point.[6]

Whichever of these two estimates best describes Marshall's technique and its tactical impact, they both agree that the *Marbury* opinion has come to draw argument as a cornflower draws bees. This condition was then compounded by what the Court did after 1803. With most questions of constitutional interpretation involving major phases of American political life—presidential powers, nation-state balances, due process, freedom of speech—the Court's initial pronouncement on the subject and its bases are examined and re-examined by later Courts. There is debate and explanation among the Justices. Yet from the day that *Marbury v. Madison* was announced, the Court adopted a strategy of silence. It simply assumed its power to review Congressional acts, as though the nation had responded to Marshall's initial formulation with universal acclaim and belief. There has been no clarification, no refinement, almost as though the Court assumed that to discuss the question at all might topple the whole edifice.

---

[6] Robert G. McCloskey, *The American Supreme Court* (Chicago: University of Chicago Press, 1960), p. 43.

Instead, the Court has invoked the cadences of inexorable, inescapable obligation. Take a typical statement of the question by one Chief Justice writing for the Court:

We are mindful of the gravity of the issue inevitably raised whenever the constitutionality of an Act of the National Legislature is challenged. . . . [But] we are oath-bound to defend the Constitution. This obligation requires that Congressional enactments be judged by the standards of the Constitution. The Judiciary has the duty of implementing the constitutional safeguards that protect individual rights. . . . The provisions of the Constitution are not time-worn adages or hollow shibboleths. They are vital, living principles that authorize and limit governmental powers in our Nation. They are the rules of government. When the constitutionality of an Act of Congress is challenged in this Court, we must apply those rules. If we do not, the words of the Constitution become little more than good advice. . . . We do well to approach the task cautiously, as all our predecessors have counseled. But the ordeal of judgment cannot be shirked.

Some may think this an opinion by Edward Douglas White, or William Howard Taft, or, at least, Charles Evans Hughes. The author happens to be Chief Justice Earl Warren, writing an opinion in 1958 with which the Supreme Court, by its own count, invalidated its 82nd Congressional provision.[7]

This leads us to still another aspect of the Court's relation to the "usurpation" debate. There has been no "left" and "right" among the Justices as to the legitimacy of judicial review. From the day when William Johnson joined the Marshall Court as President Jefferson's appointee to the arrival of Hugo Black as President Roosevelt's first appointee after the Court-battle of 1937, liberal Justices have become spokesmen for judicial review. Of course, they have often challenged the way in which the power was exercised, and many have been stout advocates of judicial self-restraint. But while Mr. Justice Black was willing to re-open the question whether the corporation should be regarded as a "person" within the protection of the Fourteenth Amendment, he has not, nor have his liberal

---

[7] *Trop v. Dulles,* 356 U.S. 86 (1958).

predecessors or colleagues, challenged judicial review of Congressional acts or revived the "departmental" theory of constitutionality. This condition was gall to President Jefferson and it has been wormwood to liberal Presidents after him.

To evaluate the impact of silence from within the Court on debate over the legitimacy of judicial review, it is useful to realize that, since the founding of the Court, every political generation in American history has had a major popular debate over the interventionist posture of the Supreme Court. Taking twenty-five years as a political generation, and starting with 1800, this phenomenon is easy to trace.

1800-1825 saw Jeffersonian alarms over the centralizing decisions of the Marshall Court.

1825-1850 heard Jacksonian protests, and the beginnings of the slavery issue in the federal courts.

1850-1875 ranged from the *Dred Scott* uproar in 1857 to the clash of the 1860's between radical Republicans and the Court over war and reconstruction.

1875-1900 featured farmer, populist, and early labor-movement protest against the "corporate bias" of the federal judiciary; 1896 was one of the four presidential campaigns during which the Court was a direct issue.

1900-1925 encompassed the progressive attack on the Supreme Court's economic doctrines, as both 1912 and 1924 produced third-party movements pledged to check an overbearing Court.

1925-1950 witnessed the New Deal's struggle with the "nine old men."

1950-present has been marked by the Court-curb crisis of 1957-1960 in which Southerners, internal security stalwarts, and some business groups have challenged the Court's trend of decisions on liberty and equality.

Thus, the doctrinal trend of the Supreme Court has been a major political issue from generation to generation in American history.

Thus, protestors in each generation have cried "usurpation" in order to shake the Court's prestige and contain its authority. And the silence within the Court has been a goad to the critics outside the Court in each generation.

So far, the discussion has centered on why the debate over judicial review of Congressional legislation (and a parallel debate over review of state laws) has continued for so long as a seemingly constant thread of our political conversation. It is important to note, however, that it has not been the same debate in each generation. A careful look at the literature on judicial review indicates that there have been three very distinctive periods, each with its own mood, rhetoric, and historical assumptions.

III. The Historiography of "Judicial Usurpation"

The Age of "Political Debate," 1790-1880

From the days of the Constitution until the 1880's, debate over Supreme Court review of Congressional acts paralleled Marshall's treatment of the issue in the *Marbury* case. The famous conservative law writers who supported the power—Kent, Story, Pomeroy, Bishop—described this authority as flowing inevitably from the Constitution and our form of government. Writing in 1833, Joseph Story in his influential *Commentaries on the Constitution of the United States* announced that the Court's employment of judicial review was approved by "the universal sense of America." A long quotation from *Marbury v. Madison* was presented as "so clear and convincing" that it would serve as a "corrective" to "those loose and extraordinary doctrines" aired on the subject from time to time.[8]

A later supporter, John N. Pomeroy, in his *Introduction to the Constitutional Law of the United States*, first published in 1868, saw the rejection of the departmental theory of constitutional judg-

---

[8] Joseph Story, *Commentaries on the Constitution of the United States*, 3rd ed., Vol. II (Boston: Little, Brown and Co., 1858), p. 431.

ment in the "calm good sense of the people" which had realized that there must "be some judge, some single umpire, to whose arbitrament the government as well as the citizen are subject." His discussion relied on arguments flowing from "the general nature of the Constitution" and such specific clauses as Article VI, section 3, making the Constitution and laws made in pursuance thereof the supreme law of the land, and Article III, section 2, extending the judicial power to all cases arising under the Constitution and the laws of the United States.[9]

At each of the crisis points in the Court's relations with Congress during this period—1821, 1833, 1857, and 1868 stand out as years in which Congressional wrath produced sustained legislative debates in Washington over the Court's decisions—cries of "usurpation" were heard from prominent critics. Usually, party spokesmen and party editors made the accusations. When they said "usurpation," they referred to the manner in which the Supreme Court was handing down "political" rulings and deciding "political questions," rather than staying within the proper "judicial" boundaries. The line between "political" and "judicial" questions was not defined with precision and sophistication. What the critics had in mind, though, were rulings which dealt with national legislative policy and matters not directly affecting the functions of the judicial branch (as had been the case in *Marbury*, for example, where the original jurisdiction of the Supreme Court was the issue involved). To cite two samples of criticism, stemming from the *Dred Scott* case, Senator Benjamin Wade of Ohio declared in 1858, "I deny the doctrine that Judges have any right to decide the law of the land for every department of this Government." [10] Senator Hannibal Hamlin of Maine commented, "This [was] a purely political question, in regard to which Thomas Jefferson so early and so ably warned us against judicial interference. [The Justices]

---

[9] John Norton Pomeroy, *An Introduction to the Constitutional Law of the United States*, 3rd ed. (New York: Hurd and Houghton, 1877), pp. 80-98.
[10] Quoted in Charles Warren, *The Supreme Court in United States History*, Vol. III (Boston: Little, Brown and Co., 1922), p. 49.

had no more authority to decide a political question for us than we had to decide a judicial question for them." [11]

The significant fact to note is that neither the supporters nor the detractors of the Court in this first era of debate went to the documentary sources, apart from a few desultory references to early state instances of judicial review. Partly, the absence of records of the Convention until Madison's notes were published in 1840 and Elliott's *Debates* appeared in 1836 explains the situation up to the 1840's. After the 1840's, this may have been a matter of the accepted mode of legal commentary, where the fashion was for textual and contextual analysis and little attention was given to drafting-process reconstruction or historical settings. Partly, the monopoly of commentary by judges and lawyers and the absence of professional historians and political scientists may have contributed to the style of analysis. Finally, the steady bite of the federal judiciary was felt primarily by the states in this era, not by Congress. Between 1793 and 1870, there were only six instances of judicial invalidation of Congressional legislation; there were two before the Civil War and four in the 1860's. By comparison, almost 100 state statutes had been declared unconstitutional by 1870, most of them under the commerce clause and obligation-of-contracts clause of the Federal Constitution. This had the effect of focusing most of the debate on "States Rights" and of producing interposition protests against judicial review of state measures. Much less debate occurred on judicial vetoes of Congressional or presidential prerogatives.

The Age of Historical Debate, 1880-1930

A variety of developments combined after 1880 to set off a history-centered debate over judicial review. The Court increased its vetoes on Congressional provisions. In the 1870's alone, more cases (nine) were decided overturning Congressional acts than in the first eighty-one years of the Court's lifetime.

Accompanying its increased interventions was a growing tone of

---

[11] *Ibid.*

royal command permeating the Court's utterances on constitutionality. Between 1857 (the *Dred Scott* case) and 1870, the Court had been at a low point of prestige. It had been ignored by Lincoln and his administration during the Civil War. It had been brushed away from review of Reconstruction issues by act of Congress in 1868, to which the Court tamely acquiesced. By the 1880's, however, national concern had turned from war and slavery crises to capitalist expansion and conservatism. The Justices became the oracles of this new conservatism. In a speech in 1887, Justice Stanley Matthews echoed the new confidence, even arrogance, of the Court in matters affecting the political branches of government. Describing the Court's responsibility to intervene as resting upon the dictates of history and the command of the Constitution, Matthews said:

Thus was cast upon the Federal judiciary the burden and duty, in the due course of judicial determination between litigant parties, of enforcing the supreme law of the land, even though it became essential, in doing so, to declare void acts of Congress and of the legislatures of the States. This is the logical necessity of liberty secured by written constitutions of governments unalterable by ordinary acts of legislation. If the prohibitions and limitations of the charters of government cannot be enforced in favor of individual rights, by the judgments of the judicial tribunals, then there are and can be no barriers against the exactions and despotism of arbitrary power; then there is and can be no guarantee or security for the rights of life, liberty, or property; then everything we hold to be dear and sacred as personal right is at the mercy of a monarch or a mob.[12]

Coinciding with the Court's increased activity and claims of preeminence was a general flowering of historical inquiry in the nation. The 1880's were centennial years for the promulgation of the Constitution and the founding of the Supreme Court. Elaborate celebrations were held and batches of essays were written on the events of 1787 and 1789. Furthermore, the 1880's were years gen-

---

[12] Hampton L. Carson, ed., *History of the Celebration of the One Hundredth Anniversary of the Promulgation of the Constitution of the United States* (Philadelphia: J. B. Lippincott Co., 1889), pp. 370-373.

erally cited as the debut of a self-conscious professional fraternity of American historians, looking not outward to Europe but inward to national development. In this decade, several major works on the constitutional period were produced, ranging from George Bancroft's magisterial two volumes, *History of the Formation of the Constitution of the United States,* issued in 1882,[13] to John F. Jameson's collection of historians' essays in 1889.[14]

On the specific question of judicial review of federal legislation, 1885 marked the publication, in the leading law journal of the day, of a pioneering essay by William M. Meigs, "The Relation of the Judiciary to the Constitution." [15] Meigs, a Philadelphia attorney who devoted much of his time to historical writing (he was the author of biographies of John C. Calhoun, Thomas H. Benton, and Charles J. Ingersoll, for example), decided to remedy what he called a curious lack of commentary on the origin and historical basis of judicial review. His article traced the consideration of this question in the Convention, assembled and evaluated the colonial and state judicial precedents, and concluded that judicial review of legislation had been planted firmly in American governmental soil well before Marshall's opinion in *Marbury.* Meigs did not end his study there, however. The major portion of his essay, based on the historical examination he had just concluded, discussed the finality of judicial review. Taking the same position which had been adopted by Robert Street in a speech before the American Bar Association in 1883 and by Bancroft in his history of the Constitution, Meigs argued that rulings of the Court involving the constitutionality of actions by the other federal departments were final and binding *only* on the parties to the specific dispute before the Court. The Congress and President retained the right to reach their own conclusions as to the constitutionality of such issues in the future.

---

[13] George Bancroft, *History of the Formation of the Constitution of the United States of America* (New York: D. Appleton and Co., 1882).

[14] John F. Jameson, *Essays on the Constitutional History of the United States in the Formative Period, 1775-1789* (Boston: Houghton, Mifflin & Co., 1889).

[15] 19 *Amer. L. Rev.* 174 (1885).

Where the Court's reasoning and judgment was persuasive and well-founded, Meigs expected Congress and the President to follow the Court's interpretation, but on its persuasive rather than its authoritative foundation.

Meigs' article set off a flurry of comments in the press and among lawyers. This coincided with popular discussion of judicial review stemming from an 1884 decision of the Supreme Court, *Julliard v. Greenman*,[16] in which eight Justices had upheld Congress' authority to make treasury notes legal tender in peacetime as well as during wars. Justice Stephen Field wrote a stinging dissent, relying heavily on Bancroft's material to show that the Framers had intended to preclude such measures. In 1886, Bancroft published a pamphlet supporting Field's dissent, *A Plea for the Constitution of the United States of America Wounded in the House of its Guardians*. Bancroft's pamphlet drew an extended reply-broadside, *Plea for the Supreme Court*, from Judge Richard McMurtrie, a distinguished Philadelphia jurist. McMurtrie's point was that if the Congress' power to issue greenbacks rested on implication only, then this was matched by the fact that the Supreme Court's power to review Congressional acts rested solely on implication. McMurtrie defended both powers, but his challenge to the express basis for judicial review attracted wide attention.

Still another stimulus in the 1880's was the publication, in 1889, of an Appendix to Volume 131 of the *United States Reports,* prepared by the Reporter of Decisions of the Supreme Court, J.C. Bancroft Davis. Davis presented, for the edification and interest of the nation, a list he prepared of twenty cases in which Congressional provisions had been held invalid and 185 in which state or territorial statutes had been held void. Davis' standards of inclusion and exclusion stirred debate almost at once. He included *Hayburn's Case*,[17] for example, in which the Supreme Court did not decide any question of constitutionality. For some reason, he

---

[16] 110 U.S. 421 (1884), also known at the *Legal Tender Cases.*
[17] 2 Dall. 409 (1792).

omitted the *Dred Scott* case.[18] And, he included such doubtful instances of early action as *United States v. Yale Todd* and *X v. Secretary of War.*[19]

By then, the conversation was spreading rapidly. Between 1890 and 1894, the law review articles were joined by discussions in the *Political Science Quarterly* and historians began to work carefully in some of the important pre-Convention aspects, such as colonial appeals to the Privy Council.[20] In 1893, James Bradley Thayer, Professor of Constitutional Law at Harvard Law School, contributed the most influential single article in the nineteenth-century literature, "The Origin and Scope of the American Doctrine of Constitutional Law," delivered as a paper at the Conference on Jurisprudence and Law Reform in Chicago and published in the *Harvard Law Review.*[21]

On the origin of judicial review, Thayer argued that this power could not be supported merely by our operating under a written constitution nor had it been a feature of state government before 1789; it had developed as a "natural" but not a "necessary" result of our political experience as colonists in framing rules to substitute "the People" for the "English sovereign." The bulk of the article was not on the founding phase but was devoted to a discussion of the scope of this power. Thayer maintained that judicial review was originally conceived of as "strictly . . . judicial"—"to determine, for the mere purpose of deciding a litigated question properly submitted to the court, whether a particular designated exercise of power was forbidden by the constitution."

In doing this, "the court was so to discharge its office as not to deprive another department of any of its proper power, or to limit it in the proper range of its discretion." Judges often recited this axiom, but by a "pedantic and academic treatment of the texts of the constitution and the laws," judges used this axiom not to re-

---

[18] *Scott v. Sanford,* 19 How. 393 (1857).
[19] See 131 U.S. Appendix for citation of these cases.
[20] See the Historical Bibliography at the end of this volume.
[21] 7 *Harv. L. Rev.* 129 (1893).

strain themselves but to support increased judicial supervision of legislation. Surveying recent trends in judicial review, Thayer concluded that courts would "imperil" the system if they sought to "step into the shoes of the law-maker."

In his closing paragraphs, Thayer struck off what has become a classic statement of the judicial self-restraint position:

I am not stating a new doctrine, but attempting to restate more exactly and truly an admitted one. If what I have said be sound, it is greatly to be desired that it should be more emphasized by our courts, in its full significance. It has been often remarked that private rights are more respected by the legislatures of some countries which have no written constitution, than by ours. No doubt our doctrine of constitutional law has had a tendency to drive out questions of justice and right, and to fill the mind of legislators with thoughts of mere legality, of what the constitution allows. And moreover, even in the matter of legality, they have felt little responsibility; if we are wrong, they say, the courts will correct it. If what I have been saying is true, the safe and permanent road towards reform is that of impressing upon our people a far stronger sense than they have of the great range of possible harm and evil that our system leaves open, and must leave open, to the legislatures, and of the clear limits of judicial power; so that responsibility may be brought sharply home where it belongs. The checking and cutting down of legislative power, by numerous detailed prohibitions in the constitution, cannot be accomplished without making the government petty and incompetent. . . . Under no system can the power of courts go far to save a people from ruin; our chief protection lies elsewhere. If this be true, it is of the greatest public importance to put the matter in its true light.[22]

Also published in 1893 was the first book-length treatment of review by the Supreme Court, *An Essay on Judicial Power and Unconstitutional Legislation,* by another Philadelphia attorney, Brinton Coxe.[23] Coxe set out to provide an "historical commentary" and a "textual commentary." The historical commentary

---

[22] *Ibid.,* pp. 155-156.
[23] Brinton Coxe, *An Essay on Judicial Power and Unconstitutional Legislation, Being a Commentary on Parts of the Constitution of the United States* (Philadelphia: Kay and Brother, 1893).

traced the development of European and British practices on judicial review before 1787, to demonstrate that judicial restraints on governmental action had been experimented with abroad and that they were known to the colonists. These points were followed by a review of instances of judicial intervention before and during the American Confederation, and by a discussion of the key sections of the Federal Constitution bearing on the judicial power, in terms of the intentions of the Convention. Coxe died before he could complete the textual commentary, but William Meigs saw to the publication of the completed portion.

Basing his view on the historical and the uncompleted textual section, Coxe advanced the basic thesis that the Framers had not left the power of judicial review to inference, even though *Marbury* implied that and commentators such as Judge McMurtrie, Professor Thayer, and others had maintained that position. Coxe argued that the Framers had provided express texts; the failure to perceive their presence was due to the fact that they were "technical legal terms" and that their special meaning had been "inadvertently overlooked." On this point, Meigs' reconstruction of Coxe's thesis in the foreword to the book provides us with the most convenient summary:

In the first place, the author examined clause 2 of Article VI [the pursuance clause] and called attention to the fact that it is *legislative*. It enacts what the law shall be, as clearly as any statute; and it must, therefore, bind all judges and all public and private persons capable of being bound; otherwise it would not be legislation. The fact that it reads that the judges of the State courts shall be bound thereby by no means confines its operation to those officials, but simply means that even they shall be bound; and it was inserted to avoid evils well known in public affairs at that time. The effect aimed at by this legislation was then more nearly approached by enacting that certain things pointed out should be the supreme law of the land, and in this connection laws unauthorized by the Constitution were excluded from this effect by use of the technical words (taken almost *verbatim* from Article 12 of the Articles of Confederation) "in pursuance thereof," by which laws not enacted in pursuance of the Constitution were excluded from the effect given to pursuant laws by the clause in question. The clause was finally perfected by the use of the words "anything in the Constitution or Laws of any State to the contrary notwithstanding." These words, also, are technical and express, and are an instance of the very well-known *non-obstante* clause, the effect of which has always been held to be to derogate to—or to repeal and make of no effect—any legislation that comes within its scope. This was very well known, and its operation seen in many instances familiar to all in 1787; and was applied directly to colonial laws by the statute of 7 and 8 William III cap 22 . . . , by virtue of which all colonial laws violating certain anterior British statutes were declared to be null and void.

Meigs continued by explaining that the "law of the land" clause in this text was also a technical term referring to "a body of laws and privileges, the right to which could only be lost by certain offenses, *and which it was particularly the duty of the judiciary to enforce,*" and that their oath of office made the law of the land their basis of decision. "Law of the land" referred to such a body of laws in each state, not in the nation. Finally, when the Constitution said this should *bind* the judges in each state, the word "bound" was used in the sense of statutes binding the King, meaning they bind "even him as well as everyone else."

The other "twin text" Coxe relied on, said Meigs, was clause 2 of Article III, extending the judicial power to judicial questions and thus to those arising under 2, VI. When put beside each other, Coxe maintained that the two clauses had force as though they were written as follows:

The judicial power (of the United States) shall extend to all cases in law and equity arising under this Constitution, the laws of the United States and all treaties made, or which shall be made, under their authority, (and) this Constitution, the laws of the United States which shall be made in pursuance thereof, and all treaties made, or which shall be made, under the authority of the United States shall be the supreme law of the land (in every State), anything in the Constitution or laws of any State to the contrary notwithstanding.

21

Between 1880 and 1895, the debate had been comparatively measured and genteel, though specific decisions such as the *Julliard* case had been, as usual, the originating cause of many commentaries. In 1895, the cadences of wrath, even of fundamental declarations of war, exploded in the literature. The cause of the explosion, of course, was the series of decisions the Court's majority issued in 1895 invalidating the federal income tax, shrinking the coverage of the Sherman Anti-Trust Act, and upholding the criminal contempt conviction of union leader Eugene Debs for his direction of the Pullman strike in violation of a federal court injunction. Sylvester Pennoyer, the vocal Populist Governor of Oregon, fired the first salvo with a sharp attack in the *American Law Review*, "The Income Tax Decision and the Power of the Supreme Court to Nullify Acts of Congress." [24] With the Court a major stump issue in the 1896 presidential campaign (the Democrats and People's Party attacked the Court, while the Republicans strongly defended it), the legal profession divided into a majority for and a vocal minority against the judiciary. The debates echoed and re-echoed through the rest of the 1890's. Publicists vied with scholars in digging through the existing sources for Convention intention and pre-Convention precedents.[25] While their tone was bitter and their own intentions were radical, the commentators between 1895 and 1900 were rather traditional in their arguments. The Founding Fathers were still revered and only their particular intent as to judicial review was disputed. For truly radical examinations of the issue, men with far less pietistic a view of the Fathers and less of a States Rights blinder would have to take up the dispute.

The "new critics" were waiting as the century turned corners. Between 1901 and 1920, these "new critics" threw down their gauntlet. They were met not only by the traditionalist-conservative defenders of the Court but also by a group that might be called the "new defenders," men whose ideology was progressive and nationalist but who would have none of the historical challenge to the

---

[24] 29 *Amer. L. Rev.* 550 (1895).
[25] See the Historical Bibliography for citations.

power of judicial review. In a very real sense, the historical debate came to a climax and was settled as a public issue in these nineteen years.

In classic fashion, 1901-1920 saw a series of assertive Supreme Court rulings which kept the flames of interest-group discontent high: *Lochner v. New York* in 1905, striking down New York's ten-hour law for bakery workers;[26] *Adair v. United States* in 1908, invalidating a federal law penalizing railroad employers who required employees to forego union affiliation;[27] and *Hammer v. Dagenhart* in 1918, striking down the federal law directed against child labor in manufacturing establishments shipping goods in interstate commerce.[28] Each was like an application of fertilizer on an already sturdy plant.

What made this a different debate from its predecessor in the 1880-1900 period were two developments. First, the historical materials were now mined in greater depth, with memoir material, newspaper comments in colonial and republican decades, and a wide range of similar data brought into play. This was a mature searching of the record, such as it was. (And, such as it was in 1901-1920, it has pretty much remained to this day. No treasure-lode of records or papers has been discovered since.) The second new feature was that this debate saw critics proposing very specific remedies in tandem with their indictment of the Court's "usurpation" of power. The critics in 1880-1894 had largely urged judicial self-restraint. The 1896 platforms of the two critical parties had proposed the traditional remedy of appointing liberal Justices and trying to dodge the Court's restrictions.

The new critics urged recall of judicial recisions by popular vote, re-passage of judicially-invalidated acts by a two-thirds vote of Congress which would preclude further judicial review, putting Justices on limited rather than life tenure, requiring two-thirds vote among the Justices for declarations of unconstitutionality,

---

[26] 198 U.S. 45 (1905).
[27] 208 U.S. 161 (1908).
[28] 247 U.S. 251 (1918).

and a variety of other institutional remedies. Usurpation had to be met by structural reform, the critics said; anything less, any reliance upon "better judges" or "public criticism," would leave the Court fastened on the nation like a barnacle.

Thus the debate waxed and thus all appealed to History and the Framers. More books and major articles on the Court's authority appeared in this nineteen-year period than in any comparable two decades in American history.[29] It was in this period that Charles Beard wrote—just once—and left a permanent blaze on the tree of "Court-debate." It was in the same era that another scholarly giant of constitutional literature—Edward S. Corwin—published several powerful essays challenging the Beard thesis, at least in some of its parts. Among the others who made these years rich with historical argumentation were Brooks Adams, James Allen Smith, Charles Grove Haines, Louis Boudin, Joseph H. Choate, Max Farrand, Arthur M. Schlesinger, Sr., and Charles Warren. The basic positions which were staked out on the question of the Court's historical warrant are discussed in Part IV of this essay. For the purposes of this narrative in Part III, the vital thread to follow is the shift of the nature of debate after 1920.

The Era of "Critical Realism," 1921-1961

The forty years from 1921 to 1961 provided three national debates over the interventionist role of the Justices. In 1924, Senator Robert La Follette made the Court a central issue in his presidential campaign as leader of the Progressive Party; the years just before and just after the election saw an outburst of literature on judicial review.[30] Reform groups like the National Association for Constitutional Government and the American Federation of Labor sponsored studies[31] probing the property-rights bias of the Justices

---

[29] See the Historical Bibliography for commentary in this period.

[30] See the Historical Bibliography for commentary in this period.

[31] Robert Von Moschzisker, *Judicial Review of Legislation* (Washington: National Association for Constitutional Government, 1923). Jackson H. Ralston, *Study and Report for the American Federation of Labor upon Judicial Control over Legislatures as to Constitutional Questions* (Washington: A.F.L., 1923).

and demonstrating that judicial review was at least as much of a political process as it was an exercise in inexorable legal logic.

When Franklin Roosevelt proposed his Court-reform plan to break what he had called the judicial "log-jam," the ensuing debate over the Court's role was, at last, given a legislative focus. Hearings were held by the Senate Judiciary Committee during March and April of 1937,[32] and most of the traditional ground of the dispute was fully plowed in the course of the testimony.

While Charles Beard did not appear as a witness, it is not too much to say that his book, *The Supreme Court and the Constitution,* was a central documentary witness presented by those supporting the Supreme Court against the Court-reform bill. Senator William H. King of Utah introduced a lengthy memorandum relying primarily upon Beard for proof that the Framers supported "the view that the Supreme Court is empowered to declare legislative acts invalid." [33] Professor Erwin Griswold of Harvard Law School, when asked by Senator M. M. Logan of Kentucky whether this was the intent of the Framers, replied that "there is no place where it is more clearly demonstrated . . . than in a little book by Mr. Charles A. Beard." [34]

In the course of testimony opposing the plan, Professor Raymond Moley, who studied under Beard at Columbia in 1915, revealed a fascinating bit of background about Beard's writing of the 1912 study. As Moley recalled it, "Professor Beard said he started out in 1912 or thereabouts to write a book to prove that Marshall and his Court arbitrarily assumed a power that the makers of the Constitution had not intended to vest in the Court. He said his research convinced him of precisely the opposite, that they had so intended." And, Moley concluded, that was what Beard made the thesis of his book.[35]

---

[32] *Reorganization of the Federal Judiciary,* Hearing before the Committee on the Judiciary, United States Senate, 75th Cong., 1st Sess., 1937.
[33] *Ibid.,* pp. 217-224.
[34] *Ibid.,* p. 772.
[35] *Ibid.,* pp. 550-551.

Perhaps the strongest challenge to Beard's "proofs" came from a very vocal witness, Beard's old challenger from 1913, Professor Edward S. Corwin of Princeton. Corwin stated that he had been reconsidering this question and had decided that his earlier reservations about the Beard thesis of clear intention by the Framers had been too mild. "I consider [it] far more a matter of doubt [now] than I did then. . . . I don't think I gave the weight that should have been given to the objections made by Dickenson and by Madison, and afterward by Charles Pinckney and by Baldwin. Now, you have there four people, all members of the Convention. You have Charles Pinckney, saying in 1799, that there was no intention to vest this power in the Court." [36] When pressed later by Senator King with Beard's statement that twenty-five members of the Convention "unequivocally expressed their acceptance" of judicial review (King's paraphrase of Beard), Corwin replied, "Well, I think that Professor Beard went a little afield for some of his evidence." To which Senator King replied that he felt "that Dr. Beard was a little too modest" in his calculations.[37]

While Senate Committees are not necessarily the final judges of scholarly truth and historical fact, it is clear that the majority of Committee members found Beard's position to be the "right" statement of the Framers' intention. In 1938, Beard republished his book with the Introduction which appears here; this is his only published comment, at any time after 1912, about his book and its critics. Professor Corwin also published a book in 1938, *Court Over Constitution*,[38] with the first and central chapter devoted to re-examination of the warrant for judicial review over Congressional acts.

The third national debate over the role of the Court took place in 1957-1960, prompted by the Supreme Court's assertive rulings in the late 1950's in matters of racial segregation, internal security,

---

[36] *Ibid.*, p. 184.
[37] *Ibid.*, p. 216.
[38] Edward S. Corwin, *Court Over Constitution* (Princeton: Princeton University Press, 1938).

criminal procedure, and federal-state relations. The Senate came rather close in 1958 to passing a bill which would have limited the Court's appellate jurisdiction in several of the subject-areas under debate. As usual, a heated literature on judicial review was quickly in print, ranging from attacks on the Court such as Rosalie M. Gordon's *Nine Men Against America*,[39] to such new defenses of the Court by liberal former-critics as Charles L. Black's *The People and the Court*.[40]

Looking over these three debates, the significant fact is that the debate over the Court was not primarily framed in terms of the original intent of the Framers, as it had been in the 1901-1920 period.[41] While critics sometimes talked about the shaky origins of judicial review, the 1924 and 1937 commentators argued primarily about the economic predilections of the nine old men; the 1958 critics condemned the "centralizing" tendencies of the post-New Deal Justices and the "sociology" which they were substituting for constitutional law. Several books in the grand manner did appear in this period, of course, such as Louis Boudin's *Government by Judiciary*[42] in 1932 and William W. Crosskey's *Politics and the Constitution in the History of the United States*[43] in 1953. But, in the new climates of legal realism, the role of Justices as policy-makers in the area of constitutional boundaries became more and more the central proposition. The wheel had come full circle.

IV. The Beard Thesis and Its Critics

Reviewing Beard's book for the *American Political Science Review* in 1913,[44] Edward S. Corwin stated, "I am not convinced

---

[39] Rosalie M. Gordon, *Nine Men Against America* (New York: Devin-Adair, 1958).

[40] Charles L. Black, Jr., *The People and the Court* (New York: The Macmillan Co., 1960).

[41] See the Historical Bibliography for publications in this period.

[42] Louis B. Boudin, *Government by Judiciary*, 2 vols. (New York: William Godwin, Inc., 1932).

[43] William W. Crosskey, *Politics and the Constitution in the History of the United States*, 2 vols. (Chicago: University of Chicago Press, 1953).

[44] 7 *Amer. Pol. Sci. Rev.* 329 (1913).

by Mr. Beard's data that the Convention of 1787 thought itself to be concluding the constitutional question decided in *Marbury v. Madison.* On the contrary I believe that the convention regarded that question as still an open one when it adjourned." Corwin went on to make the following comment about Beard's interpretation of Convention views:

Thus of the twenty-five members set down by Mr. Beard as favoring judicial review of acts of Congress seven are so classified simply on the score of their voting two years after the Convention for the Judiciary Act of 1789, the terms of which do not necessarily assume any such power, though they do not preclude it. Of another six, only utterances are quoted which postdate the Convention, sometimes by several years. Furthermore, by far the two most important members of this group are Hamilton and Madison, the former of whom apparently became a convert to the idea under discussion between the time of writing Federalist 33 and Federalist 78, and the latter of whom is proved by the very language which Mr. Beard quotes to have been unfavorable both in 1788 and 1789. Again another four are reckoned as favoring the power of judicial review proper on account of judicial utterances antedating the Convention from five to seven years, though these utterances, at the time they were made, were in one instance sharply challenged by public opinion and in the other by judicial opinion. Only eight of the twenty-five acknowledged the power on the floor of the Convention itself, and of these eight three were pretty clearly recent converts to the idea, while some of them seemed to limit the power to its use as a means of self defense by the court against legislative encroachment. On the other hand the idea was challenged by four members of the Convention; and though they were outnumbered, so far as the available record shows, two to one by the avowed advocates of judicial review, yet popular discussion previous to the Convention had shown their point of view to have too formidable backing to admit of its being crassly overridden. Despite, therefore, the sharp issue made in the Convention, not a word designed to put the view of the majority beyond the same contingencies of interpretation to which it was at the moment exposed in the state constitutions was inserted in the national constitution, though on the other hand nothing to nullify the manifest hopes of the majority was inserted either.[45]

In Corwin's estimate, judicial review developed because of a popular desire to check the abuses of legislative power which arose after 1787, and it was this political development which was its midwife, not the Constitutional Convention of 1787.

Following Corwin, a succession of critics have challenged some or all of the Beard proofs—men like Horace Davis,[46] Louis Boudin,[47] William W. Crosskey,[48] and Forrest McDonald.[49] Because so much of these criticisms rests upon an extended discussion of events, cases, men and ideas, it is impossible to quote extensively from the critics. But it is possible in this introductory essay to describe the major criticisms and indicate the bases on which they rest.

Beard's Ambiguous Use of the Term "Judicial Control"

To get his twenty-five supporters of Supreme Court review of Congressional acts, Beard states that this many members of the Convention "favored or at least accepted some form of judicial control." This obscures the fact that quite different questions of policy and politics are involved in judicial review of national legislation and in judicial review of state laws. Beard uses support of review over state laws as though such a position automatically placed its adherent in favor of the other review power. Yet many members of the Convention may have felt that, while review of state laws by the Court was essential to preserve the federal system and insure uniformity of rules, nothing was as compelling in the case of Congress or the President possessing the power to judge

[45] *Ibid.*, pp. 330-331.
[46] Horace A. Davis, *The Judicial Veto* (Boston: Houghton, Mifflin Co., 1914).
[47] Boudin, *op. cit.*
[48] Crosskey, *op. cit.*
[49] Forrest McDonald, *We The People* (Chicago: University of Chicago Press, 1958).

the constitutionality of their own measures and to stand accountable to the electorate for those judgments.

Another ambiguity which Beard presented involves the word
"control." This term obscures the difference between judicial
decisions which are final and binding on the other national branches
in cases involving the powers of those branches, and judicial
authority which is only recommendatory to the other branches.
Commentators like Bancroft and Meigs, writing before Beard, had
argued that the decisions of the Court had been intended by the
Framers to be binding only upon the parties to the case; others,
such as Chancellor Kent, had argued that the Court's rulings were
commands to the Congress and could be overcome only by the
full process of constitutional amendment. Yet Beard chose a term,
"control," which evaded this central issue and had the merit of
allowing Beard to use the expressions of Convention members who
favored either of these two quite conflicting notions of judicial
finality in decision.

A final ambiguity in Beard's operative term "judicial control" is
that it does not distinguish between judicial power to assess constitutionality when measures are presented affecting the operations of
the judicial branch itself and when the measures involve the powers
of Congress or the President. Most of the pre-Convention cases in
which state judges had been alleged to have held state laws void
had involved laws regulating the courts and judicial proceedings.
In keeping with the "departmental interpretation" theory, in
which each branch was the judge of the validity of its acts, the
Supreme Court could resist attempts by coordinate branches of the
national government to interfere with the judiciary's constitutional
duties. But this did not necessarily imply that the Court could go
beyond defense of its own prerogatives. Beard's "judicial control"
obscured this problem.

Beard's answer to these criticisms is not to be found explicitly
in his study. But it is not re-writing his book to suggest that his
answer would be that the ambiguities raised were ones which were

in the minds of the Framers; it is their mixing and melding of the possibilities which he is recording. If the distinctions suggested above had been clearly perceived and presented at the Convention, and passed upon, then the criticism of a general term like "judicial control" would be valid. But the Framers wandered about when they discussed the judicial power, and Beard felt that what mattered most was the general feeling of his twenty-five "supporters" toward the judiciary as a check on popular excess.

Beard's Use of Economic Determinism and "The Spirit of the Constitution"

In addition to his chapters analyzing the Convention of 1787 and the ratifying conventions, Beard has two chapters devoted to the economic and ideological positions of the Framers and their adherents in the nation. (Chapter 4, "The Spirit of the Constitution," and chapter 5, "The Supporters of the New Constitution.") The essence of his argument here is that the principle of "judicial control" was in perfect harmony with "the general purpose of the federal Constitution," and the motives of those who secured its adoption. These chapters represent, in truncated form, Beard's thesis that the Constitution was a document drafted by property-holding conservatives, intended to provide a governmental system favorable to their interests and their notions of the good society. In fact, these chapters read as an advance showing of Beard's most famous work, a year later, *An Economic Interpretation of the Constitution of the United States*.[50]

In a powerful presentation published in 1958, *We The People*,[51] Professor Forrest McDonald has shaken the Beard view of the economic situation in the 1780's and its effect upon the constitutional drafting process. McDonald's central thesis is that Beard's sharp division between those supporting personal property and

---

[50] Charles A. Beard, *An Economic Interpretation of the Constitution of the United States* (New York: The Macmillan Co., 1913).
[51] McDonald, *op. cit.*

those defending real property and public securities was not the essential division either in the Convention or in the ratifying process. Thus the cohesion of property-rights viewpoint on which Beard relies so heavily whenever questions arise as to the purposes or intent of the Framers has been shaken. With this, there has been a weakening of Beard's thesis as to the intent in regard to judicial review. For example, Beard asserts in Chapters 4 and 5 that a check upon populistic interference with property—as with "stay-laws" and paper-money measures—was a dominant purpose of the Convention majority and the ratification majority. Yet McDonald shows that one-fourth of the Convention delegates had actually voted for paper-money or debtor-relief laws in their state legislatures. Another fourth of the delegates, McDonald shows, held economic interests which "were adversely affected, directly and immediately, by the Constitution they helped write," particularly agricultural property. If the Framers did not function as a tightly knit group of mercantile, manufacturing, and public-security holders, then it must be said that neither did they have as conscious a purpose to erect judicial blocks to populist laws, as Beard maintained.

Again, Professor Beard would have an answer. No doubt he would say that even though he might have overstated the degree of cohesion among the Framers, his basic portrait of them as men of property still holds, and their ideological perspectives were still those of men seeking stability, consistency, and limited government. Their "spirit" was still more attuned to the Constitution as fundamental law and the Supreme Court as guardian of that law than to a departmental theory of Constitution judgment.

There are other criticisms which could be cited. One scholar maintained that Beard did not go far enough, that thirty-two to forty members of the Convention, not merely twenty-five, favored the right of the Court to hold unconstitutional laws void.[52] An-

---

[52] Frank E. Melvin, "The Judicial Bulwark of the Constitution," 8 *Amer. Pol. Sci. Rev.* 167 (1914).

other scholar, whose massive two-volume study includes the theory that James Madison's notes are at the least unreliable and probably falsified, rejects virtually all of Beard's proofs as vague, based on faulty knowledge of law, and refuted by a closer examination of the contemporary record.[53] The main challenges, however, lie in the criticisms already mentioned, and the interested student can read Beard, read the challengers, and reach his own conclusions.

V. The Prospects of Debates Over Judicial Review

No doubt the subject of whether the Framers intended the Supreme Court to review Congressional acts will continue to attract partisans and scholars in the coming decades. There will be those who hope to carry off a coup from the library stacks and change the tides of judicial power. There will be those who discuss the question in order to re-create, for present generations, the magic birth moment of an institution these commentators treasure, in order to stimulate renewed loyalties to the Court.

If there is one thing which appears certain, it is that no one will uncover a crumbling diary or set of letters, or fashion a new thesis, which will resolve this dispute once and for all. In 1990, I expect that it will still be one of the murky questions of our constitutional politics.

And in a profound sense, this is as it should be. Whether the Supreme Court is exercising a power it never was intended to have is a question which should be debated again and again because it raises the central problems of a free society—the relation between majority rule and minority rights; the balance between aristocratic and democratic values; the relation between law and politics; and the distribution of powers within the federal system. This debate should center on the wisdom with which the Court is exercising its power, but it should also return to the intention of the Framers.

---

[53] Crosskey, *op. cit.*

When we cease to debate these matters, we will be ignoring the dynamics of our system. And, while I do not urge this as a matter of historical fact, it is a bit of happy fantasy to think that the Framers deliberately left the record vague and conflicting as to judicial review, so that Americans down through the centuries would never take this power for granted.

Alan F. Westin

Columbia University
New York, N.Y.

THE SUPREME COURT

AND

THE CONSTITUTION

Introduction to the 1938 Edition

This volume was written in the midst of a controversy that raged a quarter of a century ago, and it was widely regarded as having contributed materially to the settlement of one issue in the debate, namely, the power of the Supreme Court to pass upon the validity of Acts of Congress.

At that time, a number of courts—federal and state—had declared unconstitutional several acts of legislatures. Angered by repeated checks placed upon "social legislation," sponsors of such measures, aided by Theodore Roosevelt, charged the courts, including the Supreme Court of the United States, with imposing unwarranted restraints on "the right of the people to make laws." In the course of the dispute, leaders among the foes of judicial intervention alleged that the Supreme Court in Washington had "'usurped" the power to invalidate acts of Congress on constitutional grounds.

The question was then taken up in a popular discussion characterized by no little sound and fury. While the discussion was in process, in newspapers and on platforms, the author sought a positive answer to the question in the historical documents of the men who made the Constitution. He asked himself: "What do authentic documents disclose respecting the intention of the framers in the matter of judicial power?" The results of his researches were incorporated in this work. While a few critics attacked the conclusions, readers had before them the testimony on which to base their own verdict.

For practical purposes, the book settled the controversy. At the hearings on President Franklin D. Roosevelt's proposal for the reorganization of the federal judiciary in 1937, this volume was repeatedly cited, and was apparently accepted by the Senate Committee as authoritative on the issue to which it was directed. In a very real sense, therefore, it may be viewed as a historical work, which has itself become historical. The ghost of usurpation was fairly laid. Whatever controversies may arise in the future over the exercise of judicial power, it is not likely that the historic right of the Supreme Court to pass upon acts of Congress will again be seriously challenged. If the question is raised, this work will doubtless be cited once more, as it was in 1937. So we have some warrant in describing the volume as a permanent part of our constitutional literature.

CHARLES A. BEARD

1

Attacks Upon Judicial Control

Did the framers of the federal Constitution intend that the Supreme Court should pass upon the constitutionality of acts of Congress? The emphatic negative recently given to this question by legal writers of respectable authority[1] has put the sanction of some guild members on the popular notion that the nullification of statutes by the federal judiciary is warranted neither by the letter nor by the spirit of the supreme law of the land and is, therefore, rank usurpation. Thus the color of legality, so highly prized by revolutionaries as well as by apostles of law and order, is given to a movement designed to strip the courts of their great political function. While the desirability of judicial control over legislation may be considered by practical men entirely apart from its historical origins, the attitude of those who drafted the Constitution surely cannot be regarded as a matter solely of antiquarian interest. Indeed, the eagerness with which "the views of the Fathers" have been marshalled in support of the attack upon judicial control proves

---

[1] *Cf.* Chief Justice Walter Clark, of North Carolina, Address before the Law Department of the University of Pennsylvania, April 27, 1906; reprinted in *Congressional Record*, July 31, 1911. Dean William Trickett, of the Dickinson Law School, "Judicial Dispensation from Congressional Statutes," *American Law Review*, vol. xli, pp. 65 *et seq.* L. B. Boudin, of the New York Bar, "Government by Judiciary," *Political Science Quarterly*, vol. xxvi (1911), pp. 238 *et seq.* Gilbert Roe, of the New York Bar, "Our Judicial Oligarchy" (second article), *La Follette's Weekly Magazine*, vol. iii, no. 25, pp. 7-9, June 24, 1911.

that they continue to exercise some moral weight, even if they are not binding upon the public conscience.

In an address before the Law Department of the University of Pennsylvania on April 27, 1906, the Honorable Walter Clark, Chief Justice of North Carolina, expressly declares that it was not the intention of the framers to confer upon the courts the power of passing upon the constitutionality of statutes. A proposition was made in the convention, he maintains, to confer this high power upon the judiciary and was defeated; the doctrine of judicial control had been enunciated in but a few cases before the meeting of the Convention and had been strongly disapproved by the people; the action of the Supreme Court in assuming the power to declare an act of Congress void was without a line in the Constitution to authorize it either expressly or by implication; and had the Convention intended to give the courts this power, it would not have left its exercise unreviewable and final.

To state the case in Mr. Justice Clark's own language:

A proposition was made in the convention—as we now know from Mr. Madison's Journal—that the judges should pass upon the constitutionality of acts of Congress. This was defeated June 5, receiving the vote of only two States. It was renewed no less than three times, i.e., on June 6, July 21, and finally again for the fourth time on August 15; and, though it had the powerful support of Mr. Madison and Mr. James Wilson, at no time did it receive the votes of more than three States. On this last occasion (August 15) Mr. Mercer thus summed up the thought of the convention: He disapproved of the doctrine that the judges, as expositors of the Constitution, should have authority to declare a law void. He thought laws ought to be well and cautiously made, and then to be incontrovertible.

Prior to the convention, the courts of four States—New Jersey, Rhode Island, Virginia, and North Carolina—had expressed an opinion that they could hold acts of the legislature unconstitutional. This was a new doctrine never held before (nor in any other country since) and met with strong disapproval. In Rhode Island the movement to remove the offending judges was stopped only on a suggestion that they could be "dropped" by the legislature at the annual election, which was done. The decisions of these four State courts were recent and well known to the convention. Mr. Madison and Mr. Wilson favored the new doctrine of the paramount judiciary, doubtless deeming it a safe check upon legislation, since it was to be operated only by lawyers. They attempted to get it into the Federal Constitution in its least objectionable shape—the judicial veto before final passage of an act, which would thus save time and besides would enable the legislature to avoid the objections raised. But even in this diluted form, and though four times presented by these two very able and influential members, this suggestion of a judicial veto at no time received the votes of more than one-fourth of the States.

The subsequent action of the Supreme Court in assuming the power to declare acts of Congress unconstitutional was without a line in the Constitution to authorize it, either expressly or by implication. The Constitution recited carefully and fully the matters over which the courts should have jurisdiction, and there is nothing, and after the above vote four times refusing jurisdiction, there could be nothing, indicating any power to declare an act of Congress unconstitutional and void.

Had the convention given such power to the courts, it certainly would not have left its exercise final and unreviewable. It gave Congress power to override the veto of the President, though that veto was expressly given, thus showing that in the last analysis the will of the people, speaking through the legislative power, should govern. Had the convention supposed the courts would assume such power, it would certainly have given Congress some review over judicial action and certainly would not have placed the judges irretrievably beyond "the consent of the governed" and regardless of the popular will by making them appointive, and further clothing them with the undemocratic prerogative of tenure for life.

Such power does not exist in any other country, and never has. It is therefore not essential to our security. It is not conferred by the Constitution; but, on the contrary, the convention, as we have seen, after the fullest debate, four times, on four several days, refused by a decisive vote to confer such power. The judges not only have never exercised such power in England, where there is no written constitution, but they do not exercise it in France, Germany, Austria, Denmark, or in any other country which, like them, has a written constitution.

A more complete denial of popular control of this Government could not have been conceived than the placing of such unreviewable power in the hands of men not elected by the people and holding office for life. The legal-tender act, the financial policy of the Government, was invalidated by one court and then validated by another, after a change in its personnel. Then the income tax, which had been held constitutional by the court for a hundred years, was again so held, and then by a sudden change of vote by one judge it was held unconstitutional, nullified, and set at naught, though it had passed by a nearly unanimous vote both Houses of Congress, containing many lawyers who were the equals, if not the superiors, of the vacillating judge, and had been approved by the President[1] and voiced the will of the people. This was all negatived (without any warrant in the Constitution for the court to set aside an act of Congress) by vote of one judge; and thus $100,000,000 and more of annual taxation was transferred from those most able to bear it and placed upon the backs of those who already carried more than their fair share of the burdens of government. Under an untrue assumption of authority given by 39 dead men one man nullified the action of Congress and the President and the will of 75,000,000 of living people, and in the 13 years since has taxed the property and labor of the country, by his sole vote, $1,300,000-000, which Congress . . . . had decreed should be paid out of the excessive incomes of the rich.

In England one-third of the revenue is derived from the superfluities of the very wealthy by the levy of a graduated income tax and a graduated inheritance tax, increasing the per cent. with the size of the income. The same system is in force in all other civilized countries. In not one of them would the hereditary monarch venture to veto or declare null such a tax. In this country alone the people, speaking through their Congress and with the approval of their Executive, can not put in force a single measure of any nature whatever with assurance that it shall meet with the approval of the courts; and its failure to receive such approval is fatal, for, unlike the veto of the Executive, the unanimous vote of Congress (and the income tax came near receiving such vote) can not prevail against it. Of what avail shall it be if Congress shall conform to the popular demand and enact a "rate-regulation" bill and the President shall approve it if five lawyers, holding office for life and not elected by the people, shall see fit to destroy it, as they did the in-

---

[1] Cleveland did not, in fact, sign the bill.

come-tax law? Is such a government a reasonable one, and can it be longer tolerated after 120 years of experience have demonstrated the capacity of the people for self-government? If five lawyers can negative the will of 100,000,000 of men, then the art of government is reduced to the selection of those five lawyers.

A power without limit, except in the shifting views of the court, lies in the construction placed upon the fourteenth amendment, which, passed, as everyone knows, solely to prevent discrimination against the colored race, has been construed by the court to confer upon it jurisdiction to hold any provision of any statute whatever "not due process of law." This draws the whole body of the reserved rights of the States into the maelstrom of the Federal courts, subject only to such forbearance as the Federal Supreme Court of the day, or in any particular case, may see fit to exercise. The limits between State and Federal jurisdiction depend upon the views of five men at any given time; and we have a government of men, and not a government of laws, prescribed beforehand.

At first the court generously exempted from its veto the police power of the several States. But since then it has proceeded to set aside an act of the Legislature of New York restricting excessive hours of labor, which act had been sustained by the highest court in that great State. Thus labor can obtain no benefit from the growing humanity of the age, expressed by the popular will in any State if such statute does not meet the views of five elderly lawyers, selected by influences naturally antagonistic to the laboring classes and whose training and daily associations certainly can not incline them in favor of restrictions upon the power of the employer.

The preservation of the autonomy of the several States and of local self-government is essential to the maintenance of our liberties, which would expire in the grasp of a consolidated despotism. Nothing can save us from this centripetal force but the speedy repeal of the fourteenth amendment or a recasting of its language in terms that no future court can misinterpret.

The vast political power now asserted and exercised by the court to set aside public policies, after their full determination by Congress, can not safely be left in the hands of any body of men, without supervision or control by any other authority whatever. If the President errs, his mandate expires in four years, and his party as well as himself is accountable to the people at the ballot box for his stewardship. If Members of Congress err, they, too, must account to their constituents. But the Federal judiciary hold for life and, though popular sentiment should change the entire personnel of the other two great departments of government, a whole generation must pass away before the people could get control of the judiciary, which possesses an irresponsible and unrestricted veto upon the action of the other departments—irresponsible because impeachment has become impossible, and if it were possible it could not be invoked as to erroneous decisions unless corruption were shown.

The control of the policy of government is thus not in the hands of the people, but in the power of a small body of men not chosen by the people, and holding for life. In many cases which might be mentioned, had the court been elective, men not biased in favor of colossal wealth would have filled more seats upon the bench, and if there had been such decision as in the income-tax case, long ere this, under the tenure of a term of years, new incumbents would have been chosen, who, returning to the former line of decisions, would have upheld the right of Congress to control the financial policy of the Government in accordance with the will of the people of this day and age, and not according to the shifting views which the court has imputed to language used by the majority of the 55 men who met in Philadelphia in 1787. Such methods of controlling the policy of a government are no whit more tolerable than the conduct of the augurs of old who gave the permission for peace or war, for battle or other public movements, by declaring from the flight of birds, the inspection of the entrails of fowls, or other equally wise devices, that the omens were lucky or unlucky—the rules of such divination being in their own breasts and hence their decisions beyond remedy.

It may be that this power in the courts, however illegally grasped originally, has been too long acquiesced in to be now questioned. If so, the only remedy which can be applied is to make the judges elective, and for a term of years, for no people can permit its will to be denied, and its destinies shaped, by men it did not choose, and over whose conduct it has no control, by reason of its having no power to change them and select other agents at the close of a fixed term.

Dean William Trickett, of the Dickinson Law School, in an eloquent and almost vehement article in the *American Law Review* contends that "if the courts possess the power to declare acts of Congress void, they owe it, not to the intention of the makers of the Constitution, but to what Chief Justice Gibson has termed 'necessity,' which seems to be another name for their own desire." The author uses the term "makers" here to mean the members of the conventions of the states who ratified the instrument framed at Philadelphia; and of course his entire argument rests upon silence, for he does not contend that the conventions reviewed the proposition and decided against it. Perhaps it never occurred to him to inquire what sort of a federal Constitution we should have if the clearly ascertained intention of the "makers" were necessary to the decision of any single point! On the intention of the framers of the Constitution—which from the legal standpoint is, of course, another matter, Dean Trickett is scarcely less decided. After bringing under review the few cases in which state courts had held invalid state statutes previous to the convention of 1787, he continues:

The convention was composed of fifty-five members. Of these thirty-nine signed the Constitution. There is nothing better than a surmise that ten of these gentlemen knew anything of the decisions. Of those who knew, we have no evidence that more than five or six regarded the annulment of statutes a judicial function. We know that Spaight and three or four others[1] did not regard it as such. Shall we assume that the members of the Convention whose sentiment is unknown were divided in the same ratio? It would be sheer imbecility to infer from the preponderance of the numbers who have spoken for, over those who have spoken against, a measure or view, when four times as many as both of these classes of speakers have remained silent, that a majority of the members shared the view of the major part of the speakers.

Of course Dean Trickett does not categorically deny that the majority of the Convention regarded the annulment of statutes as a normal judicial function; but he so minimizes the actual evidence in the matter as to prejudice his readers strongly against any such view.

A more recent critic of the judiciary, Mr. L. B. Boudin, speaks with less reserve than Dean Trickett on the point:

---

[1] He does not name them or cite authorities.

There were undoubtedly some men in the Convention who favored the investing of the federal judiciary with general revisory powers over legislation; but all attempts to make the judiciary part of the legislative power of the federal government failed signally and had to be abandoned by their sponsors. The provisions of the Constitution as they now stand contain no reference whatever to any such powers, either expressly or by obvious implication. And there is ample historical proof that—whatever the hopes of some, from the complete silence of the document, as to possible future development —the great majority of the framers never suspected that a general power of the judiciary to control legislation could be interpreted into the new Constitution. They evidently assumed that such extraordinary power could not be exercised unless expressly granted.

The "ample historical proof" which Mr. Boudin mentions is not cited by him, and if he has made the researches himself, he gives no hint as to his methods, sources, and authorities.

Mr. Gilbert Roe, member of the New York Bar, in an article in *La Follette's Weekly Magazine,* claims that it was not the intention of the framers to vest judicial control over legislation in the Supreme Court. He says:

It can not well be contended that the framers of the Constitution *assumed* that the courts would exercise such supervisory power over legislation as they now lay claim to. The debates in the Convention negative any such idea, as does the fact that the attempt to exercise such power by the state courts over state statutes had been sharply rebuked by the people.

In support of this contention Mr. Roe cited the efforts made in the convention to associate the judges with the executive in the exercise of the revisionary powers, and quotes the remarks of Mercer and Dickinson presented below. How fragmentary and inconclusive this evidence really is will be shown later.

The arguments advanced by these critics to show that the framers of the Constitution did not intend to grant to the federal judiciary any control over federal legislation may be summarized as follows. Not only is the power in question not expressly granted, but it could not have seemed to the framers to be granted by implication.

The power to refuse application to an unconstitutional law was not generally regarded as proper to the judiciary. In a few cases only had state courts attempted to exercise such a power, and these few attempts had been sharply rebuked by the people. Of the members of the Convention of 1787 not more than five or six are known to have regarded this power as a part of the general judicial power; and Spaight and three or four others are known to have held the contrary opinion. It cannot be assumed that the other forty-odd members of the Convention were divided on the question in the same proportion. If any conclusion is to be drawn from their silence, it is rather that they did not believe that any such unprecedented judicial power could be read into the Constitution. This conclusion is fortified by the fact that a proposition to confer upon the federal judges revisory power over federal legislation was four times made in the Convention and defeated.

A careful examination of the articles cited fails to reveal that the writers have made any detailed analysis of the sources from which we derive our knowledge of the proceedings of the Convention and of the views held by its members. They certainly do not produce sufficient evidence to support their sweeping generalizations. In the interest of historical accuracy, therefore, it is well to inquire whether the evidence available on the point is sufficient to convict the Supreme Court of usurping an authority which the framers of the Constitution did not conceive to be within the judicial province. If the opinions of the majority of the Convention cannot be definitely ascertained, any categorical answer to the question proposed must rest upon the "argument of silence," which, as Fustel de Coulanges warned the Germans long ago, is a dangerous argument.

2

The Constitutional Convention
of 1787 and Judicial Control

No proposition to confer directly upon the judiciary the power of passing upon the constitutionality of acts of Congress was submitted to the Convention. On this point a statement made in Chief Justice Clark's address, cited above, is misleading. The proposition to which he refers, and which formed a part of the Randolph plan, was to associate a certain number of the judges with the executive in the exercise of a revisionary power over laws passed by Congress. This is obviously a different proposition. Indeed, some members of the Convention who favored judicial control opposed the creation of such a council of revision. The question of judicial control, accordingly, did not come squarely before the Convention, in such form that a vote could be taken on it.

How are we to know what was the intention of the framers of the Constitution in this matter? The only method is to make an exhaustive search in the documents of the Convention and in the writings, speeches, papers and recorded activities of its members. It is obviously impossible to assert that any such inquiry is complete, for new material, printed or in manuscript, may be produced at any moment. This essay therefore makes no claim to finality. It is designed to throw light on the subject and to suggest ways in which more light may be obtained.

There were in all fifty-five members of the Convention who were present at some of its meetings. Of these at least one-third took little or no part in the proceedings or were of little weight or were extensively absent. Among these may be included: Blount, Brearley, Broom, Clymer, Fitzsimons, Gilman, W. C. Houston, William Houstoun, Ingersoll, Lansing, Livingston, McClurg, Alexander Martin, Mifflin, Pierce and Yates. It is of course difficult to estimate the influence of the several members of the Convention, and between the extremes there are a few regarding whom there may reasonably be a difference of opinion. The preceding list is doubtless open to criticism, but it may be safely asserted that a large majority of the men included in it were without any considerable influence in the framing of the Constitution.

Of the remaining members there were (say) twenty-five whose character, ability, diligence and regularity of attendance, separately or in combination, made them the dominant element in the Convention. These men were:

Blair	Franklin	*King*	*Morris, R.*	Rutledge
Butler	*Gerry*	*Madison*	*Paterson*	Sherman
Dayton	Gorham	*Martin, L.*	Pinckney, Charles	*Washington*
Dickinson	Hamilton	*Mason*	Pinckney, C. C.	*Williamson*
Ellsworth	*Johnson*	*Morris, G.*	*Randolph*	*Wilson*

This list, like the one given above, is tentative; and it is fair to say that, among those whose judgment is entitled to respect, there is no little difference of opinion about the weight of some of the men here enumerated. It can not be doubted, however, that the list includes the decided majority of the men who were most influential in giving the Constitution its form and its spirit. Among these men were the leaders, of whose words and activities we have the fullest records.

Of these men, the seventeen whose names are italicized declared, directly or indirectly, for judicial control. Without intending to imply that the less influential members were divided on the question in the same ratio as these twenty-five, or that due respect should not be paid to the principle of simple majority rule, it is illuminating to discover how many of this dominant group are found on record in favor of the proposition that the judiciary would in the natural course of things pass upon the constitutionality of acts of Congress. The evidence of each man's attitude is here submitted, the names being arranged, as above, in their alphabetical order.

John Blair, of Virginia, was a member of the Virginia court of appeals which decided the case of Commonwealth *v.* Caton,[1] in 1782, and he agreed with the rest of the judges "that the court had power to declare any resolution or act of the legislature, or of either branch of it, to be unconstitutional and void." [2] Ten years later he was one of the three judges of the federal circuit court for the district of Pennsylvania who claimed that they could not perform certain duties imposed upon them by a law of Congress, because the duties were not judicial in nature and because under the law their acts would be subject to legislative or executive control. These judges—Blair, Wilson[3] and Peters—joined in a respectful letter of protest to President Washington, April 18, 1792, in which they declared that they held it to be their duty to disregard the directions of Congress rather than to act contrary to a constitutional principle.[4] It may also be noted that, as a member of the federal Senate, Blair supported the Judiciary Act of 1789, which accorded to the Supreme Court the power to review and reverse or affirm the decisions of state courts denying the validity of federal statutes.[5]

John Dickinson, of Delaware, is usually placed among the members of the Convention who did not recognize the power of the courts to pass upon the constitutionality of statutes; for in the debate on August 15, just after Mercer[6] declared against judicial

---

[1] Thayer, *Cases in Constitutional Law,* vol. i. p. 55.

[2] That the decision could have been reached without invoking this power, as Mr. Boudin argues, *loc. cit.,* p. 245, note 1, does not affect the value of the decision as evidence of Blair's belief in the existence of the power.

[3] Wilson, as we shall see later, had taken a strong stand, both in the constituent Convention and in the ratifying Pennsylvania convention, in favor of judicial control of legislation. *Cf. infra,* pp. 14, 26.

[4] Hayburn's Case, 2 Dallas, 409.

[5] *Cf. infra,* p. 44.

[6] *Cf. infra,* p. 52.

control, Dickinson said that "he was strongly impressed with the remark of Mr. Mercer as to the power of the Judges to set aside the law. He thought no such power ought to exist. He was at the same time at a loss what expedient to substitute." [1] Later, however, he accepted the principle of judicial control, either because he thought it sound or because he could find no satisfactory substitute. In one of his "Fabius" letters, written in advocacy of the Constitution in 1788, he says:

In the senate the sovereignties of the several states will be equally represented; in the house of representatives the people of the whole union will be equally represented; and in the president and the federal independent judges, so much concerned in the execution of the laws and in the determination of their constitutionality, the sovereignties of the several states and the people of the whole union may be considered as conjointly represented. [2]

Whatever his personal preference may have been, he evidently understood that the new instrument implicitly empowered the federal judiciary to determine the constitutionality of laws; and he presents this implication to the public as a commendable feature of the Constitution.

Oliver Ellsworth, of Connecticut, held that the federal judiciary, in the discharge of its normal functions, would declare acts of Congress contrary to the federal Constitution null and void. In the Connecticut convention, called to ratify the federal Constitution, he was careful to explain this clearly to the assembled delegates. [3] Later, he was chairman of the Senate committee which prepared the Judiciary Act of 1789 and he took a leading part in the drafting and passage of that measure. [4]

Elbridge Gerry, of Massachusetts. When, on June 4, the proposition relative to a council of revision was taken into consideration by the Convention, Gerry expressed doubts

---

[1] Farrand, *Records of the Federal Convention,* vol. ii, p. 299.
[2] Ford, *Pamphlets on the Constitution of the United States,* p. 184.
[3] *Cf. infra,* p. 71.
[4] *Cf. infra,* p. 44.

whether the Judiciary ought to form a part of it, as they will have a sufficient check against encroachments on their own department by their exposition of the laws, which involved a power of deciding on their constitutionality. In some States the Judges had actually set aside laws as being against the Constitution. This was done, too, with general approbation. It was quite foreign from the nature of the office to make them judges of the policy of public measures.[1]

During the debate in the first Congress on the question whether the president had the constitutional right to remove federal officers without the consent of the Senate, Gerry more than ouce urged that the judiciary was the proper body to decide the issue finally. On June 16, 1789, he said:

Are we afraid that the President and Senate are not sufficiently informed to know their respective duties? . . . . If the fact is, as we seem to suspect, that they do not understand the Constitution, let it go before the proper tribunal; the judges are the constitutional umpires on such questions.[2]

Speaking on the same subject again, he said:

If the power of making declaratory acts really vests in Congress and the judges are bound by our decisions, we may alter that part of the Constitution which is secured from being amended by the first article; we may say that the ninth section of the Constitution, respecting the migration or importation of persons, does not extend to negroes; that the word persons means only white men and women. We then proceed to lay a duty of twenty or thirty dollars per head on the importation of negroes. The merchant does not construe the Constitution in the manner that we have done. He therefore institutes a suit and brings it before the supreme judicature of the United States for trial. The judges, who are bound by oath to support the Constitution, declare against this law; they would therefore give judgment in favor of the merchant.[3]

Alexander Hamilton, of New York. In Number 78 of *The Federalist,* written in defence of the Constitution, and designed to

---

[1] Farrand, vol. i, p. 97.
[2] *Annals of Congress,* vol. i, p. 491.
[3] Elliot's *Debates,* vol. iv, p. 393.

make that instrument acceptable to the electorate, Hamilton gave a full exposition of his view of the new system. His statement of the principle of judicial control so thoroughly covers the ground that it deserves quotation at length:

The complete independence of the courts of justice is peculiarly essential in a limited constitution. By a limited constitution I understand one which contains certain specified exceptions to the legislative authority; such, for instance, as that it shall pass no bills of attainder, no *ex post facto laws*, and the like. Limitations of this kind can be preserved in practice no other way than through the medium of the courts of justice; whose duty it must be to declare all acts contrary to the manifest tenor of the Constitution void. Without this, all the reservations of particular rights or privileges would amount to nothing.

Some perplexity respecting the right of the courts to pronounce legislative acts void, because contrary to the Constitution, has arisen from an imagination that the doctrine would imply a superiority of the judiciary to the legislative power. It is urged that the authority which can declare the acts of another void must necessarily be superior to the one whose acts may be declared void. As this doctrine is of great importance in all the American constitutions, a brief discussion of the grounds on which it rests can not be unacceptable.

There is no position which depends on clearer principles than that every act of a delegated authority contrary to the tenor of the commission under which it is exercised is void. No legislative act, therefore, contrary to the Constitution, can be valid. To deny this would be to affirm that the deputy is greater than his principal; that the servant is above his master; that the representatives of the people are superior to the people themselves; that men, acting by virtue of powers, may do not only what their powers do not authorize, but what they forbid.

If it be said that the legislative body are themselves the constitutional judges of their own powers, and that the construction they put upon them is conclusive upon the other departments, it may be answered that this can not be the natural presumption, where it is not to be collected from any particular provisions in the Constitution. It is not otherwise to be supposed that the Constitution could intend to enable the representatives of the people to substitute their will to that of their constituents. It is far more rational to suppose that the courts were designed to be an intermediate body between the people and the legislature, in order, among other things, to keep the latter within the limits assigned to their authority. The interpretation of the laws is the proper and peculiar province of the courts. A constitution is, in fact, and must be, regarded by the judges as a fundamental law. It must therefore belong to them to ascertain its meaning, as well as the meaning of any particular act proceeding from the legislative body. If there should happen to be an irreconcilable variance between the two, that which has the superior obligation and validity ought, of course, to be preferred; in other words, the constitution ought to be preferred to the statute, the intention of the people to the intention of their agents.

Nor does this conclusion by any means suppose a superiority of the judicial to the legislative power. It only supposes that the power of the people is superior to both; and that where the will of the legislature, declared in its statutes, stands in opposition to that of the people, declared in the Constitution, the judges ought to be governed by the latter, rather than the former. They ought to regulate their decisions by the fundamental laws, rather than those which are not fundamental.

This exercise of judicial discretion, in determining between two contradictory laws, is exemplified in a familiar instance. It not uncommonly happens that there are two statutes existing at one time, clashing in whole or in part with each other, and neither of them containing any repealing clause or expression. In such a case it is the province of the courts to liquidate and fix their meaning and operation: So far as they can by any fair construction be reconciled to each other, reason and law conspire to dictate that this should be done: Where this is impracticable it becomes a matter of necessity to give effect to one, in exclusion of the other. The rule which has obtained in the courts for determining their relative validity is that the last in order of time shall be preferred to the first. But this is a mere rule of construction, not derived from any positive law, but from the nature and reason of the thing. It is a rule not enjoined upon the courts by legislative provision, but adopted by themselves, as consonant to truth and propriety, for the direction of their conduct as interpreters of the law. They thought it reasonable that, between the interfering acts of an equal authority, that which was the last indication of its will should have the preference.

But in regard to the interfering acts of a superior and subordinate authority, of an original and derivative power, the nature and reason of the thing indicate the converse of that rule as proper to be followed. They teach us that the prior act of a superior ought to be preferred to the subsequent act of an inferior and subordinate authority; and that, accordingly, whenever a particular statute contravenes the Constitution, it will be the duty of the judicial tribunals to adhere to the latter and disregard the former.

It can be of no weight to say that the courts, on the pretence of a repugnancy, may substitute their own pleasure to the constitutional intentions of the legislature. This might as well happen in the case of two contradictory statutes; or it might as well happen in every adjudication upon any single statute. The courts must declare the sense of the law; and if they should be disposed to exercise Will instead of Judgment, the consequence would equally be the substitution of their pleasure to that of the legislative body. The observation, if it prove anything, would prove that there ought to be no judges distinct from that body.

If then the courts of justice are to be considered as the bulwarks of a limited constitution against legislative encroachments, this consideration will afford a strong argument for the permanent tenure of judicial offices, since nothing will contribute so much as this to that independent spirit in the judges which must be essential to the faithful performance of so arduous a duty.

This independence of the judges is equally requisite to guard the Constitution and the rights of individuals from the effects of those ill humors which the arts of designing men, or the influence of particular conjunctures, sometimes disseminate among the people themselves and which, though they speedily give place to better information and more deliberate reflection, have a tendency, in the mean time, to occasion dangerous innovations in the government and serious oppressions of the minor party in the community. Though I trust the friends of the proposed Constitution will never concur with its enemies in questioning that fundamental principle of republican government which admits the right of the people to alter or abolish the established Constitution whenever they find it inconsistent with their happiness; yet it is not to be inferred from this principle that the representatives of the people, whenever a momentary inclination happens to lay hold of a majority of their constituents incompatible with the provisions in the existing Constitution, would, on that account, be justifiable in a violation of

53

those provisions; or that the courts would be under a greater obligation to connive at infractions in this shape than when they had proceeded wholly from the cabals of the representative body. Until the people have, by some solemn and authoritative act, annulled or changed the established form, it is binding upon themselves collectively, as well as individually; and no presumption, or even knowledge, of their sentiments can warrant their representatives in a departure from it, prior to such an act. But it is easy to see that it would require an uncommon portion of fortitude in the judges to do their duty as faithful guardians of the Constitution where legislative invasions of it had been instigated by the major voice of the community.

But it is not with a view to infractions of the Constitution only that the independence of the judges may be an essential safeguard against the effects of occasional ill humors in the society. These sometimes extend no farther than to the injury of the private rights of particular classes of citizens, by unjust and partial laws. Here also the firmness of the judicial magistracy is of vast importance in mitigating the severity and confining the operation of such laws. It not only serves to moderate the immediate mischiefs of those which may have been passed, but it operates as a check upon the legislative body in passing them; who, perceiving that obstacles to the success of an iniquitous intention are to be expected from the scruples of the courts, are in a manner compelled, by the very motives of the injustice they meditate, to qualify their attempts. This is a circumstance calculated to have more influence upon the character of our governments than but a few may be aware of. The benefits of the integrity and moderation of the judiciary have already been felt in more states than one; and though they may have displeased those whose sinister expectations they may have disappointed, they must have commanded the esteem and applause of all the virtuous and disinterested. Considerate men, of every description, ought to prize whatever will tend to beget or fortify that temper in the courts; as no man can be sure that he may not be to-morrow the victim of a spirit of injustice, by which he may be a gainer to-day. And every man must now feel that the inevitable tendency of such a spirit is to sap the foundations of public and private confidence, and to introduce in its stead universal distrust and distress.

That inflexible and uniform adherence to the rights of the Constitution, and of individuals, which we perceive to be indispensable in the courts of justice, can certainly not be expected from judges who hold their offices by a temporary commission. Periodical appointments, however regulated, or by whomsoever made, would, in some way or other, be fatal to their necessary independence. If the power of making them was committed either to the executive or legislature, there would be danger of an improper complaisance to the branch which possessed it: if to both, there would be an unwillingness to hazard the displeasure of either; if to the people, or to persons chosen by them for the special purpose, there would be too great a disposition to consult popularity to justify a reliance that nothing would be consulted but the Constitution and the laws.

Rufus King, of Massachusetts. In the discussion of the proposed council of revision which took place in the Convention on June 4, King took the same position as Gerry, observing "that the judges ought to be able to expound the law as it should come before them free from the bias of having participated in its formation." [1] According to Pierce's notes he said that he

was of opinion that the judicial ought not to join in the negative of a law because the judges will have the expounding of those laws when they come before them; and they will no doubt stop the operation of such as shall appear repugnant to the constitution. [2]

James Madison, of Virginia. That Madison believed in judicial control over legislation is unquestionable, but as to the exact nature and extent of that control he was in no little confusion. His fear of the legislature is expressed repeatedly in his writings, and he was foremost among the men who sought to establish a revisionary council of which the judges should form a part. In the Convention he said

Experience in all the states has evinced a powerful tendency in the legislature to absorb all power into its vortex. This was the real source of danger to the American consitutions; and suggested the necessity of giving every defensive authority to the other departments that was consistent with republican principles. [3]

---

[1] Farrand, vol. i, p. 98.
[2] *Ibid.,* p. 109.
[3] Farrand, vol. ii, p. 74.

The association of the judges with the executive, he contended, "would be useful to the judiciary department by giving it an additional opportunity of defending itself against legislative encroachments."[1] He was evidently greatly disappointed by the refusal of the Convention to establish a revisionary council; for, in after years, he said that "such a control, restricted to constitutional points, besides giving greater stability and system to the rules of expounding the instrument would have precluded the question of a judiciary annulment of legislative acts."[2]

From the first, however, he accepted judicial control only with limitations; and complete judicial paramountcy over the other branches of the federal government he certainly deprecated. When it was proposed to extend the jurisdiction of the Supreme Court to cases arising under the Constitution as well as under the laws of the United States, he

doubted whether it was not going too far to extend the jurisdiction of the court generally to cases arising under the Constitution and whether it ought not to be limited to cases of a judiciary nature. The right of expounding the Constitution in cases not of this nature ought not to be given to that department.[3]

The refusal of the Convention to establish a council of revision, in his opinion, left the judiciary paramount, which was in itself undesirable and not intended by the framers of the Constitution. In a comment on the proposed Virginia constitution of 1788 he wrote, in that year:

In the state constitutions and indeed in the federal one also, no provision is made for the case of a disagreement in expounding them [the laws], and as the courts are generally the last making the decision, it results to them, by refusing or not refusing to execute a law, to stamp it with its final character. This makes the Judiciary Department paramount in fact to the Legislature, which was never intended and can never be proper.[4]

---

[1] *Ibid.*
[2] *Writings of James Madison,* vol. viii, p. 406.
[3] Farrand, vol. ii, p. 430.
[4] *Writings,* vol. v, pp. 293, 294.

The right of the courts to pass upon constitutional questions in cases of a judicial nature he fully acknowledged; but this did not, in his mind, preclude the other departments from declaring their sentiments on points of constitutionality and from marking out the limits of their own powers. This view he expressed in the House of Representatives (first Congress) when the question of the President's removing power was under debate:

The great objection . . . is that the legislature itself has no right to expound the Constitution; that wherever its meaning is doubtful, you must leave it to take its course, until the judiciary is called upon to declare its meaning. I acknowledge, in the ordinary course of government, that the exposition of the laws and Constitution devolves upon the judicial; but I beg to know upon what principle it can be contended that any one department draws from the Constitution greater powers than another, in marking out the limits of the powers of the several departments. The Constitution is the charter of the people in the government; it specifies certain great powers as absolutely granted, and marks out the departments to exercise them. If the constitutional boundary of either be brought into question I do not see that any one of these independent departments has more right than another to declare their sentiments on that point.

Perhaps this is an admitted case. There is not one government on the face of the earth, so far as I recollect—there is not one in the United States—in which provision is made for a particular authority to determine the limits of the constitutional division of power between the branches of the government. In all systems there are points which must be adjusted by the departments themselves, to which no one of them is competent. If it cannot be determined in this way, there is no resource left but the will of the community, to be collected in some mode to be provided by the Constitution, or one dictated by the necessity of the case. It is, therefore, a fair question, whether this great point may not as well be decided, at least by the whole legislature, as by part—by us, as well as by the executive or the judicial. As I think it will be equally constitutional, I cannot imagine it will be less safe that the exposition should issue from the legislative authority than any other; and the more so, because it involves in the decision the opinions of both of those departments whose powers are supposed to be affected by it. Besides. I do not see in what way this question could come before the judges to obtain a fair and solemn decision: but even if it were the case that it could, I should suppose, at least while the government is not led by passion, disturbed by faction, or deceived by any discolored medium of sight, but while there is a desire in all to see and be guided by the benignant ray of truth, that the decision may be made with the most advantage by the legislature itself.[1]

Madison's view on the point may be summed up as follows: In cases of a political nature involving controversies between departments, each department enjoys a power of interpretation for itself (a doctrine which Marshall would not have denied); in controversies of a judicial nature arising under the Constitution the Supreme Court is the tribunal of last resort; in cases of federal statutes which are held to be invalid by nullifying states the Supreme Court possesses the power to pass finally upon constitutionality.[2]

Luther Martin, of Maryland, although he opposed the proposition to form a revisionary council by associating judges with the executive, was nevertheless firmly convinced that unconstitutional laws would be set aside by the judiciary. During the debate on July 21 he said:

A knowledge of mankind and of Legislative affairs cannot be presumed to belong in a higher degree to the Judges than to the legislature. And as to the constitutionality of laws, that point will come before the judges in their proper official character. In this character they have a negative on the laws. Join them with the executive in the revision and they will have a double negative. It is necessary that the supreme judiciary should have the confidence of the people. This will soon be lost, if they are employed in the task of remonstrating against popular measures of the legislature.[3]

George Mason, of Virginia, favored associating the judges with the executive in revising laws. He recognized that the judges would

---

[1] Elliot's *Debates,* vol. iv, pp. 382, 383.

[2] *Cf.* Madison's letter of August, 1830, to Everett; *Writings,* vol. ix, p. 383.

[3] Farrand, vol. ii, p. 76. For further evidence of Martin's attitude, *cf. infra,* p. 70.

have the power to declare unconstitutional statutes void, but he regarded this control as insufficient. He said:

Notwithstanding the precautions taken in the constitution of the legislature, it would so much resemble that of the individual states, that it must be expected frequently to pass unjust and pernicious laws. This restraining power was therefore essentially necessary. It would have the effect not only of hindering the final passage of such laws, but would discourage demagogues from attempting to get them passed. It had been said (by Mr. L. Martin) that if the judges were joined in this check on the laws, they would have a double negative, since in their expository capacity of judges they would have one negative. He would reply that in this capacity they could impede in one case only the operation of laws. They could declare an unconstitutional law void. But with regard to every law, however unjust, oppressive or pernicious, which did not come plainly under this description, they would be under the necessity as judges to give it a free course. He wished the further use to be made of the judges of giving aid in preventing every improper law. Their aid will be the more valuable as they are in the habit and practice of considering laws in their true principles, and in all their consequences.[1]

Gouverneur Morris, of Pennsylvania, declared, in the debate on July 21, that some check on the legislature was necessary; and he "concurred in thinking the public liberty in greater danger from legislative usurpations than from any other source."[2] He was apprehensive lest the addition of the judiciary to the executive in the council of revision would not be enough to hold the legislature in check. Later, when Dickinson questioned the right of the judiciary to set aside laws, Morris said:

He could not agree that the judiciary, which was a part of the executive, should be bound to say that a direct violation of the Constitution was law. A control over the legislature might have its inconveniences. But view the danger on the other side. . . . En-

---

[1] Farrand, vol. ii, p. 78.
[2] *Ibid.,* pp. 75 *et seq.*

croachments of the popular branch of the government ought to be guarded against.[1]

This view he later confirmed in the debate on the repeal of the Judiciary Act of 1801, when he said:

It has been said, and truly too, that governments are made to provide against the follies and vices of men. . . . Hence checks are required in the distribution of the power among those who are to exercise it for the benefit of the people. Did the people of America vest all power in the Legislature? No; they had vested in the judges a check intended to be efficient—a check of the first necessity, to prevent an invasion of the Constitution by unconstitutional laws —a check which might prevent any faction from intimidating or annihilating the tribunals themselves.[2]

William Paterson, of New Jersey. There is perhaps no finer statement of the doctrine of judicial control than that made by Paterson as Associate Justice of the Supreme Court in the case of Van Horne's Lessee *v.* Dorrance (2 Dallas 304) decided in 1795. In this case the litigant's title to property depended upon the validity of an act of the State of Pennsylvania and in rendering the opinion Justice Paterson inquired whether the legislature had the power to enact the law in question under the constitution of the commonwealth. He cited the famous passage from Blackstone on the sovereign power and jurisdiction of Parliament and compared that body with our limited legislatures. He said, in the course of his long opinion:

It is evident that in England the authority of the Parliament runs without limits and rises above control. It is difficult to say what the constitution of England is, because, not being reduced to written certainty and precision, it lies entirely at the mercy of the Parliament: It bends to every governmental exigency; it varies and is blown about by every breeze of legislative humor or political caprice. Some of the judges in England have had the boldness to assert that an act of Parliament, made against natural equity, is

---

[1] Farrand, p. 299.

[2] Benton, *Abridgment of Debates in Congress,* vol. ii, p. 550.

void; but this opinion contravenes the general position, that the validity of an act of Parliament cannot be drawn into question by the judicial department: It cannot be disputed, and must be obeyed. The power of Parliament is absolute and transcendent; it is omnipotent in the scale of political existence. Besides, in England there is no written constitution, no fundamental law, nothing visible, nothing real, nothing certain, by which a statute can be tested. In America the case is widely different: Every State in the Union has its Constitution reduced to written exactitude and precision.

What is a Constitution? It is the form of government, delineated by the mighty hand of the people, in which certain first principles of fundamental laws are established. The Constitution is certain and fixed; it contains the permanent will of the people, and is the supreme law of the land; it is paramount to the power of the legislature, and can be revoked or altered only by the authority that made it. The life-giving principle and the death-doing stroke must proceed from the same hand. What are legislatures? Creatures of the Constitution; they owe their existence to the Constitution: they derive their powers from the Constitution. It is their commission; and, therefore, all their acts must be conformable to it, or else they will be void. The Constitution is the work or will of the people themselves, in their original, sovereign, and unlimited capacity. Law is the work or will of the legislature in their derivative and subordinate capacity. The one is the work of the Creator, and the other of the creature. The Constitution fixes limits to the exercise of legislative authority and prescribes the orbit within which it must move. In short, the Constitution is the sun of the political system, around which all legislative, executive and judicial bodies must revolve. Whatever may be the case in other countries, yet in this there can be no doubt, that every act of the legislature repugnant to the Constitution is absolutely void.

In the second article of the Declaration of Rights, which was made part of the late Constitution of Pennsylvania, it is declared, "That all men have a natural and unalienable right to worship Almighty God, according to the dictates of their own consciences and understanding; and that no man ought or of right can be compelled to attend any religious worship, or erect or support any place of worship, or maintain any ministry, contrary to, or against, his own free will and consent; nor can any man who acknowledges the being of a God be justly deprived or abridged of any civil right as a citizen, on account of his religious sentiments, or peculiar mode of religious worship; and that no authority can, or ought to be, vested in, or assumed by, any power whatever, that shall, in any case, interfere with, or in any manner control, the right of conscience in the free exercise of religious worship." (Dec. of Rights, Art. 2.)

In the thirty-second section of the same Constitution it is ordained: "that all elections, whether by the people or in general assembly, shall be by ballot, free and voluntary." (Const. Penn., Sect. 32.)

Could the legislature have annulled these articles, respecting religion, the rights of conscience, and elections by ballot? Surely no. As to these points there was no devolution of power; the authority was purposely withheld, and reserved by the people to themselves. If the legislature had passed an act declaring that, in future, there should be no trial by jury, would it have been obligatory? No: It would have been void for want of jurisdiction, or constitutional extent of power. The right of trial by jury is a fundamental law, made sacred by the Constitution, and cannot be legislated away. The Constitution of a State is stable and permanent, not to be worked upon by the temper of the times, nor to rise and fall with the tide of events: notwithstanding the competition of opposing interests, and the violence of contending parties, it remains firm and immovable, as a mountain amidst the strife of storms, or a rock in the ocean amidst the raging of the waves. I take it to be a clear position that if a legislative act oppugns a constitutional principle the former must give way, and be rejected on the score of repugnance. I hold it to be a position equally clear and sound that, in such case, it will be the duty of the court to adhere to the Constitution, and to declare the act null and void. The Constitution is the basis of legislative authority; it lies at the foundation of all law, and is a rule and commission by which both legislators and judges are to proceed. It is an important principle, which, in the discussion of questions of the present kind, ought never to be lost sight of, that the judiciary in this country is not a subordinate, but co-ordinate branch of the government. . . .

Edmund Randolph, of Virginia, does not seem to have expressed himself in the Convention on the subject of judicial control over congressional legislation. In the plan which he presented, however, provision was made for establishing a council of revision, composed of the executive and a convenient number of the judiciary, "with authority to examine every act of the National Legislature before it shall operate." He must, therefore, have been convinced of the desirability of some efficient control over the legislative department. Subsequently, as attorney-general, when it became his duty to represent the government in Hayburn's case[1] and he was moving for a *mandamus* to compel the circuit court for the district of Pennsylvania to execute a law under which the judges had declined to act on the ground of its unconstitutionality, Randolph accepted the view of the judges that they were not constitutionally bound to enforce a law which they deemed beyond the powers of Congress. The meager abstract of his argument before the Supreme Court in Dallas's *Reports* gives no hint of its precise character; but in a letter to Madison, dated August 12, 1792, Randolph said: "The sum of my argument was an admission of the power to refuse to execute, but the unfitness of the occasion." [2] That he approved the provision of the Judiciary Act of 1789, giving the Supreme Court appellate jurisdiction to review and reverse or affirm a decision of a state court denying the constitutionality of a federal statute, is apparent from his report to Congress on the judicial system in 1790. After enumerating the instances in which cases might be carried up to the Supreme Court from the state courts, he says: "That the avenue to the federal courts ought, in these instances, to be unobstructed is manifest." The only question with which he was concerned was: "In what stage and by what form shall their interposition be prayed?" [3]

Hugh Williamson, of North Carolina, certainly believed in judicial control over federal legislation; for, in the debate on the proposition to insert a clause forbidding Congress to pass *ex post facto* laws, he said: "Such a prohibitory clause is in the constitution of North Carolina, and, though it has been violated, it has done good there and may do good here, because the judges can take hold

---

[1] 2 Dallas, 409.
[2] Moncure Conway, *Edmund Randolph,* p. 145.
[3] *American State Papers,* Class X, Miscellaneous, vol. i, p. 23.

of it." [1] It is obvious that the only way in which the judges can "take hold of" *ex post facto* laws is by declaring them void.

James Wilson, of Pennsylvania, expressed himself in favor of judicial control in the course of the debate on July 21, when the proposition to associate the national judiciary with the executive in the revisionary power was again being considered. He declared:

The Judiciary ought to have an opportunity of remonstrating against projected encroachments on the people as well as on themselves. It had been said that the Judges as expositors of the Laws would have an opportunity of defending their constitutional rights. There was weight in this observation; but this power of the Judges did not go far enough. Laws may be unjust, may be unwise, may be dangerous, may be destructive; and yet not be so unconstitutional as to justify the Judges in refusing to give them effect. Let them have a share in the Revisionary power, and they will have an opportunity of taking notice of these characters of a law, and of counteracting, by the weight of their opinions, the improper views of the Legislature. [2]

Speaking again, on August 23, in favor of giving the national legislature a negative over state legislation, he said that he

considered this as the keystone wanted to complete the wide arch of Government we are raising. The power of self-defence had been urged as necessary for the State Governments. It was equally necessary for the General Government. The firmness of Judges is not of itself sufficient. Something further is requisite. It will be better to prevent the passage of an improper law than to declare it void when passed. [3]

The rejection of the plan to establish a revisionary council did not lead Wilson to infer that thereby the right of the court to pass upon the constitutionality of statutes was denied. On the contrary, in the debates in the Pennsylvania ratifying convention he declared that the proposed Constitution empowered the judges to declare unconstitutional enactments of Congress null and void. [4]

---

[1] Farrand, vol. ii, p. 376.

[2] Farrand, vol. ii, p. 73.

[3] *Ibid.*, p. 391.

[4] *Cf. infra*, p. 71.

Examination of the speeches, papers and documents of the influential members of the Convention enumerated above fails to disclose any further direct declarations in favor of the principle of judicial review of legislation. However, there is reasonably satisfactory evidence that three other members of this group understood and indorsed the doctrine.

William Johnson, of Connecticut, *Robert Morris,* of Pennsylvania, and *George Washington.* The evidence of their opinions is their approval of the Judiciary Act of 1789. Section 25 of that act provided:

A final judgment or decree in any suit, in the highest court of law or equity of a state in which a decision in the suit could be had, where is drawn in question the validity of a treaty or statute of, or an authority exercised under, the United States, and the decision is against their validity; . . . or where is drawn in question the construction of any clause of the Constitution, or of a treaty or statute of, or commission held under, the United States, and the decision is against the title, right, privilege or exemption specially set up or claimed by either party, under such clause of the said Constitution, treaty, statute or commission,—may be reëxamined and reversed or affirmed in the Supreme Court of the United States upon a writ of error.

In other words: the Supreme Court may review and affirm a decision of a state court holding unconstitutional a statute of the United States. It surely is not unreasonable to assume that the men who established this rule believed that the Supreme Court could declare acts of Congress unconstitutional independently of decisions in lower state courts. Indeed, it would seem absurd to assume that an act of Congress might be annulled by a state court with the approval of the Supreme Court, but not by the Supreme Court directly.

William Johnson and Robert Morris were members of the first Senate and voted in favor of the Judiciary Act;[1] and Washington, as president, approved the measure.

In addition to these eminent members of the Convention who

---

[1] *Annals of Congress,* vol. i, p. 51.

directly or indirectly supported the doctrine of judicial control over legislation there were several members of minor influence who seem to have understood and approved it. There is direct or indirect evidence in the following cases.

Abraham Baldwin, of Georgia, had no generous faith in the probity of a legislature based on a widely extended suffrage. In speaking on the composition of the Senate, on June 29, he said: "He thought the second branch ought to be the representation of property, and that in forming it, therefore, some reference ought to be had to the relative wealth of their constituents and to the principles on which the Senate of Massachusetts was constituted." [1] Baldwin does not seem to have spoken on the subject of the judicial control in the Convention; but two years later, on June 19, 1789, he participated in the discussion of the bill constituting the Department of Foreign Affairs. The point at issue was whether the President could remove alone or only with the consent of the Senate; and some members of the House of Representatives held that this was a judicial question. To this Baldwin replied:

Gentlemen say it properly belongs to the Judiciary to decide this question. Be it so. It is their province to decide upon our laws and if they find this clause to be unconstitutional, they will not hesitate to declare it so; and it seems to be a very difficult point to bring before them in any other way. Let gentlemen consider themselves in the tribunal of justice called upon to decide this question on a *mandamus.* What a situation! almost too great for human nature to bear, they would feel great relief in having had the question decided by the representatives of the people. Hence, I conclude, they also will receive our opinion kindly.[2]

Here is a direct statement that it is the duty of the judges to pass upon the constitutionality of statutes; and the statute in question was not one involving an encroachment upon the sphere of the judiciary but one touching the respective powers of the President and Senate. Baldwin here seems to think, however, that the Court

---

[1] Farrand, vol. i, p. 469.
[2] *Annals of Congress,* vol. i, p. 582.

would, and ought to, receive with gratitude the expressed opinion of the House of Representatives. Such an opinion, he evidently thought, would aid the judges in reaching a decision but would not be binding upon them. In his later years, however, after the struggle between the Federalists and the Jeffersonians for the control of the national government had begun, Baldwin appears to have retracted his earlier view; for in a debate in the Senate concerning the powers of the presidential electors, in January, 1800, he said:

Suppose either of the other branches of the government, the Executive or the Judiciary or even Congress, should be guilty of taking steps which are unconstitutional, to whom is it submitted or who has control over it except by impeachment? The Constitution seems to have equal confidence in all the branches on their own proper ground, and for either to arrogate superiority, or a claim to greater confidence, shows them in particular to be unworthy of it, as it is in itself directly unconstitutional.[1]

It is small wonder that Baldwin thought the powers of the judiciary one of the questions that the Convention had left unsettled;[2] but his clear statement on June 19, 1789, may reasonably be taken to represent his understanding of the power conferred on the judiciary by the Constitution. At that time, at least, he believed it a function of the judiciary to pass upon the constitutionality of statutes.

Richard Bassett, of Delaware, was a member of the Senate committee which introduced the Judiciary Act of 1789, and he voted for the measure.[3] Bassett was also one of Adams's Federalist judges, appointed under the act of February 13, 1801; and when the Jeffersonians repealed the law he joined several of his colleagues in a protest against the repeal, on the ground that it was an impairment of the rights secured to them as judicial officers under the Constitution. In a memorial to Congress the deposed judges declared that they were:

---

[1] Farrand, vol. iii, p. 383.
[2] *Ibid.*, p. 370. *Cf. infra*, p. 66.
[3] *Annals of Congress*, vol. i, pp. 18, 51.

compelled to represent it as their opinion that the rights secured to them by the Constitution, as members of the judicial department, have been impaired. . . . The right of the undersigned to their compensation . . . involving a personal interest, will cheerfully be submitted to judicial examination and decision, in such manner as the wisdom and impartiality of Congress may prescribe.[1]

The memorialists proposed that their rights should be decided by the judicial department; and such a decision would have involved an inquiry regarding the constitutionality of the repeal of the Judiciary Act of 1801.[2] That Bassett believed the repeal unconstitutional, as to the abolition of his judicial functions and salary, and held the judiciary to be the proper authority for deciding the point, is quite evident.

George Wythe, of Virginia, was a member of the Virginia court of appeals which decided the case of Commonwealth *v.* Caton[3] in 1782. Justice Wythe, in his opinion, referred to the practice of certain English chancellors, who had defended the rights of subjects against the rapacity of the crown, and exclaimed:

If the whole legislature, an event to be deprecated, should attempt to overleap the bounds prescribed to them by the people, I, in administering the public justice of the country, will meet the united powers at my seat in this tribunal; and, pointing to the Constitution, will say to them, here is the limit of your authority and hither shall you go but no further.

The duty of a court to declare unconstitutional laws void could hardly be more energetically asserted. Of course this is not direct evidence that Wythe held that the federal Constitution embodied the principle, but it is clear that he favored the doctrine.

William Few, of Georgia, *George Read,* of Delaware, and *Caleb Strong,* of Massachusetts, who were members of the first Senate

---

[1] *American State Papers,* Class X, Miscellaneous, vol. i, p. 340.

[2] A proposition to make provision for submitting the case to judicial determination was defeated in the House on January 27, 1803. *Annals of Congress,* Second Session, 7th Congress, p. 439.

[3] Thayer's *Cases,* vol. i, p. 55. *Cf. supra,* p. 18.

under the new government, voted for the Judiciary Act[1] and may therefore, for the reasons indicated above, be regarded as having accepted the principle of the judicial review of federal statutes.

Summing up the evidence: we may say that of the leading members of the Convention no less than fourteen believed that the judicial power included the right and duty of passing upon the constitutionality of acts of Congress. Satisfactory evidence is afforded by the vote on the Judiciary Act that three other leading members held to the same belief. Of the less prominent members, we find that three expressed themselves in favor of judicial control and three others approved it by their vote on the Judiciary Act. We are justified in asserting that twenty-five[2] members of the Convention favored or at least accepted some form of judicial control. This number understood that federal judges could refuse to enforce unconstitutional legislation.

We may now turn to the evidence that judicial control was not regarded by the framers of the Constitution as a normal judicial function under the new system. The researches of those who contend that the doctrine propounded in Marbury v. Madison is sheer usurpation have placed only four members of the Convention on record against judicial control; and one of these, John Dickinson, of Delaware, must be stricken from the list.[3] The evidence in the case of the remaining three members is as follows:

Gunning Bedford, of Delaware, speaking in the Convention on June 4 on the subject of the executive veto, expressed himself as opposed to every check on the legislative, even the council of revision first proposed. He thought it would be sufficient to mark out in the Constitution the boundaries to the legislative authority, which

---

[1] *Annals of Congress,* vol. i, p. 51. *Cf. supra,* p. 44.

[2] To the twenty-three members here enumerated must be added Brearley and Livingston, of New Jersey, who, through their connection with the early case of Holmes v. Walton, went on record as understanding and approving the doctrine of judicial review. See *The American Historical Review,* vol. iv, pp. 460, 468. I am indebted to Professor A. C. McLaughlin for calling my attention to this reference.

[3] *Cf. supra,* p. 20.

would give all the requisite security to the rights of the other departments. The representatives of the people were the best judges of what was for their interest and ought to be under no external controul whatever. The two branches would produce a sufficient controul within the legislature itself.[1]

John F. Mercer, of Maryland. On August 15 Madison moved that all acts, before they became laws, should be submitted to both the executive and supreme judiciary departments and, upon being vetoed by either or both of these departments, be repassed only by extraordinary majorities. Mercer heartily approved the motion. It is an axiom that the judiciary ought to be separate from the legislative; but equally so that it ought to be independent of that department. The true policy of the axiom is that legislative usurpation and oppression may be obviated. He disapproved of the doctrine that the judges as expositors of the Constitution should have authority to declare a law void. He thought laws ought to be well and cautiously made and then to be uncontroulable.[2] Mercer evidently feared "legislative oppression," and when the motion to have acts submitted to the judiciary before they should become laws was rejected, he may have changed his mind on the subject of judicial control. However that may be, he stands on record as distinctly disapproving the doctrine.

Richard Spaight, of North Carolina, was undoubtedly opposed to judicial control over legislation, although he does not appear to have said anything on the subject in the constitutional Convention. In the spring of 1787 the superior court of North Carolina, in the case of Bayard *v.* Singleton, declared an act of the legislature of that state null and void on the ground that it was not warranted by the Constitution of the Commonwealth. The decision aroused much popular opposition and Spaight joined in the protest against the action of the court. In a letter dated Philadelphia, August 12, 1787, and directed to Mr. Iredell, Spaight wrote:

---

[1] Farrand, vol. i, p. 100.
[2] *Ibid.,* vol. ii, p. 298.

I do not pretend to vindicate the law which has been the subject of controversy; it is immaterial what law they have declared void; it is their usurpation of the authority to do it that I complain of, as I do most positively deny that they have any such power; nor can they find anything in the Constitution, either directly or impliedly, that will support them, or give them any color of right to exercise that authority. Besides it would have been absurd, and contrary to the practice of all the world, had the Constitution vested such power in them as would have operated as an absolute negative on the proceedings of the legislature, which no judiciary ought ever to possess. . . .

He further declared that "many instances might be brought to show the absurdity and impropriety of such power being lodged in the judges." He was aware, he explained, of the desirability of a check on the legislature, but he thought an annual election the best that could be devised.[1]

Pierce Butler, of South Carolina, and *John Langdon*, of New Hampshire, were members of the first Senate of the new Union, and both voted against the Judiciary Act of 1789.[2] Their reasons for so voting are not apparent; and it may be questioned whether a vote cast against the act as a whole is evidence of opposition to the principle of judicial control over federal legislation recognized in the twenty-fifth section of the act. If, however, these two names be added, the list of opponents of judicial control contains five members of the Convention, and but one of the five, Butler, belonged to the influential group. Mr. Boudin lays much stress on the silence of those who disliked judicial control of legislation. He says:

It is absurd to assume that the many avowed opponents of judicial control of legislation who sat in the convention would have agreed to the [judiciary] article without a murmur had they suspected that it contained even a part of the enormous power which our judiciary now exercises. Richard Spaight for one, whose fiery denunciation of this power I have quoted above, would have made the halls in

---

[1] Coxe, *An Essay on Judicial Power*, pp. 248 *et seq.* and 385.
[2] *Annals of Congress*, vol. i, p. 51.

which the Convention met ring to the echo with his emphatic protest, had he suspected any such implications.[1]

The "avowed opponents" do not seem to have been "many"; but whether they and the unavowed opponents were many or few, they must have been fully aware that most of the leading members regarded the nullification of unconstitutional laws as a normal function. The view was more than once clearly voiced in the Convention, and any delegate who was not aware of such implications must have been very remiss in the discharge of his duties.

On June 4 King definitely stated that the judges in the exposition of the laws would no doubt stop the operation of such as appeared repugnant to the Constitution.[2] On that day there were present representatives from Massachusetts, Connecticut, New York, Pennsylvania, Delaware, Maryland, Virginia, North Carolina, South Carolina and Georgia. In addition to members in the group of twenty-five enumerated above there were recorded as present on that occasion Bedford, McClurg, Pierce and Yates.[3] Several other members, including Spaight, were in Philadelphia at the time and were probably in attendance at that particular session, but as there was no preliminary roll call the list of those actually present must be made up from those who addressed the Convention or appeared in the roll on a divided vote, or from an outside source.

The proposition to associate the federal judges with the executive in controlling acts of Congress was again brought up in the Convention by Mr. Wilson on July 21st and again defeated. The following extracts are from Madison's notes of the debates on this occasion.[4]

Mr. Wilson moved, as an amendment to the tenth Resolution, "that the Supreme National Judiciary should be associated with the Executive in the revisionary power." This proposition had been before made and failed; but he was so confirmed by reflection in the opinion of its utility that he thought it incumbent on him

---

[1] *Loc. cit.*, pp. 248, 249.
[2] Farrand, vol. i, p. 109.
[3] Farrand, vol. i, pp. 96 ff.
[4] *Madison Papers,* vol. ii, p. 1161 ff.; Farrand, vol. ii, pp. 22 ff.

to make another effort. The judiciary ought to have an opportunity of remonstrating against projected encroachments on the people as well as on themselves. It had been said that the judges, as expositors of the laws, would have an opportunity of defending their constitutional rights. There was weight in this observation; but this power of the judges did not go far enough. Laws may be unjust, may be unwise, may be dangerous, may be destructive; and yet not be so unconstitutional as to justify the judges in refusing to give them effect. Let them have a share in the revisionary power, and they will have an opportunity of taking notice of these characters of a law, and of counteracting, by the weight of their opinions, the improper views of the Legislature.—Mr. Madison seconded the motion.

Mr. Gorham did not see the advantage of employing the judges in this way. As judges they are not to be presumed to possess any peculiar knowledge of the mere policy of public measures. Nor can it be necessary as a security for their constitutional rights. The judges in England have no such additional provision for their defence, yet their jurisdiction is not invaded. He thought it would be best to let the executive alone be responsible, and at most to authorize him to call on judges for their opinions.

Mr. Ellsworth approved heartily of the motion. The aid of the judges will give more wisdom and firmness to the executive. They will possess a systematic and accurate knowledge of the laws, which the executive cannot be expected always to possess. The law of nations also will frequently come into question. Of this the judges alone will have competent information.

Mr. Madison considered the object of the motion as of great importance to the meditated Constitution. It would be useful to the judiciary department by giving it an additional opportunity of defending itself against legislative encroachments. It would be useful to the executive, by inspiring additional confidence and firmness in exerting the revisionary power. It would be useful to the Legislature, by the valuable assistance it would give in preserving a consistency, conciseness, perspicuity, and technical propriety in the laws, qualities peculiarly necessary, and yet shamefully wanting in our Republican codes. It would, moreover, be useful to the community at large, as an additional check against a pursuit of those unwise and unjust measures which constituted so great a portion of our calamities. If any solid objection could be urged against the motion, it must be on the supposition that it tended to give too much strength, either to the executive or judiciary. He did not think there was the least ground for this apprehension. It was much more to be apprehended, that, notwithstanding this coöperation of the two departments, the Legislature would still be an over-match for them. Experience in all the States had evinced a powerful tendency in the Legislature to absorb all power into its vortex. This was the real source of danger to the American Constitutions; and suggested the necessity of giving every defensive authority to the other departments that was consistent with republican principles.

Mr. Mason said he had always been a friend to this provision. It would give a confidence to the executive which he would not otherwise have, and without which the revisionary power would be of little avail.

Mr. Gerry did not expect to see this point, which had undergone full discussion, again revived. The object he conceived of the revisionary power was merely to secure the executive department against legislative encroachment. The executive, therefore, who will best know and be ready to defend his rights, ought alone to have the defence of them. The motion was liable to strong objections. It was combining and mixing together the legislative and the other departments. It was establishing an improper coalition between the executive and judiciary departments. It was making statesmen of the judges, and setting them up as the guardians of the rights of the people. He relied, for his part, on the representatives of the people as the guardians of their rights and interests. It was making the expositors of the laws the legislators, which ought never to be done. A better experiment for correcting the laws would be to appoint, as had been done in Pennsylvania, a person or persons of proper skill, to draws bills for the Legislature.

Mr. Strong thought, with Mr. Gerry, that the power of making ought to be kept distinct from that of expounding, the laws. No maxim was better established. The judges in exercising the function of expositors might be influenced by the part they had taken, in framing the laws.

Mr. Gouverneur Morris. Some check being necessary on the Legislature, the question is, in what hands should it be lodged? On one side, it was contended that the executive alone ought to exercise it. He did not think that an executive appointed for six years, and impeachable while in office, would be a very effectual check. On the other side, it was urged, that he ought to be reinforced by the judiciary department. Against this it was objected that expositors of the laws ought to have no hand in making them, and arguments in favor of this had been drawn from England. What weight was due to them might be easily determined by an attention to facts. The truth was that the judges in England had a great share in the legislation. They are consulted in difficult and doubtful cases. They may be, and some of them are, members of the Legislature. They are, or may be, members of the Privy Council; and can there advise the executive, as they will do with us if the motion succeeds. The influence the English judges may have, in the latter capacity, in strengthening the executive check, cannot be ascertained, as the King, by his influence, in a manner dictates the laws. There is one difference in the two cases, however, which disconcerts all reasoning from the British to our proposed Constitution. The British executive has so great an interest in his prerogatives, and such powerful means of defending them, that he will never yield any part of them. The interest of our executive is so inconsiderable and so transitory, and his means of defending it so feeble, that there is the justest ground to fear his want of firmness in resisting encroachments. He was extremely apprehensive that the auxiliary firmness and weight of the judiciary would not supply the deficiency. He concurred in thinking the public liberty in greater danger from legislative usurpations than from any other source. It had been said that the Legislature ought to be relied on, as the proper guardians of liberty. The answer was short and conclusive. Either bad laws will be pushed, or not. On the latter supposition, no check will be wanted. On the former, a strong check will be necessary. And this is the proper supposition. Emissions of paper money, largesses to the people, a remission of debts, and similar measures, will at some time be popular, and will be pushed for that reason. At other times, such measures will coincide with the interests of the Legislatures themselves, and that will be a reason not less cogent for pushing them. It may be thought that the people will not be deluded and misled in the latter case. But experience teaches another lesson. The press is indeed a great means of diminishing the evil; yet it is found to be unable to prevent it altogether.

Mr. L. Martin considered the association of the judges with the executive as a dangerous innovation; as well as one that could not produce the particular advantage expected from it. A knowledge of mankind, and of legislative affairs, cannot be presumed to belong in a higher degree to the judges than to the Legislature. And as to the constitutionality of laws, that point will come before the judges in their official character. In this character they have a negative on the laws. Join them with the executive in the revision, and they will have a double negative. It is necessary that the Supreme Judiciary should have the confidence of the people. This will soon be lost, if they are employed in the task of remonstrating against popular measures of the Legislature. Besides, in what mode and proportion are they to vote in the Council of Revision?

Mr. Madison could not discover in the proposed association of the judges with the executive, in the revisionary check on the Legislature, any violation of the maxim which requires the great departments of power to be kept separate and distinct. On the contrary, he thought it an auxiliary precaution, in favor of the maxim. If a constitutional discrimination of the departments on paper were a sufficient security to each other against encroachments of the others, all further provisions would indeed be superfluous. But experience had taught us a distrust of that security; and that it is necessary to introduce such a balance of powers and interests as will guarantee the provisions on paper. Instead, therefore, of contenting ourselves with laying down the theory in the Constitution that each department ought to be separate and distinct, it was proposed to add a defensive power to each, which should maintain the theory in practice. In so doing, we did not blend the departments together. We erected effectual barriers for keeping them separate. The most regular example of this theory was in the British Constitution. Yet it was not only the practice there to admit the judges to a seat in the Legislature, and in the Executive Councils, and submit to their previous examination all laws of a certain description, but it was a part of their Constitution that the executive might negative any law whatever; a part of their Constitution which had been universally regarded as calculated for the preservation of the whole. The objection against the union of the judiciary and executive branches, in the revision of the laws, had either no foundation, or was not carried far enough. If such a union was an improper mixture of powers, or such a judiciary check on the laws was inconsistent with the theory of a free constitution, it was equally so to admit the executive to any participation in the making of laws; and the revisionary plan ought to be discarded altogether.

Colonel Mason observed that the defence of the executive was not the sole object of the revisionary power. He expected even greater advantages from it. Notwithstanding the precautions taken in the constitution of the Legislature, it would still so much re-semble that of the individual States that it must be expected fre-quently to pass unjust and pernicious laws. This restraining power was therefore essentially necessary. It would have the effect, not only of hindering the final passage of such laws, but would dis-courage demagogues from attempting to get them passed. It has been said (by Mr. L. Martin) that if the judges were joined in this check on the laws they would have a double negative, since in their expository capacity of judges they would have one negative. He would reply that in this capacity they could impede, in one case only, the operation of laws. They could declare an unconstitutional law void. But with regard to every law, however unjust, oppressive or pernicious, that did not come plainly under this description, they would be under the necessity, as judges, to give it a free course. He wished the further use to be made of the judges of giving aid in preventing every improper law. Their aid will be the more valuable, as they are in the habit and practice of considering laws in their true principles, and in all their consequences. . . .

In view of these discussions and the evidence adduced above, it cannot be assumed that the Convention was unaware that the judi-cial power might be held to embrace a very considerable control over legislation and that there was a high degree of probability (to say the least) that such control would be exercised in the ordi-nary course of events.

The accepted canons of historical criticism warrant the assump-tion that, when a legal proposition is before a law-making body and a considerable number of the supporters of that proposition definitely assert that it involves certain important and fundamental implications, and it is nevertheless approved by that body without any protests worthy of mention, these implications must be deemed part of that legal proposition when it becomes law; provided, of course, that they are consistent with the letter and spirit of the instrument. To go further than this—to say that the convention must have passed definitely upon every inference that could logically be drawn from the language of the instrument that it adopted— would of course be absurd.

77

In balancing conflicting presumptions in order to reach a judgment in the case, it must be remembered that no little part of the work of drafting the Constitution was done by the Committee of Detail and the Committee of Style.

The former committee, appointed on July 24, consisted of Rutledge, Wilson, Ellsworth, Randolph and Gorham. Of these five men two, Ellsworth and Wilson, had expressly declared themselves in favor of judicial control, and Wilson seems to have been the "dominating mind of the committee." This committee had before it the resolutions referred to it by the Convention on July 23. It had also before it the Pinckney plan, or an outline of it, and the New Jersey plan. The members of the committee had been assiduous in their attendance upon the debates during the two months previous, and they prepared a draft of a constitution which they presented to the Convention on August 6. The article dealing with federal judicial power, as reported by the committee,[1] contained most of the provisions later embodied in the federal Constitution.

After lengthy debates on the draft submitted by the Committee of Detail, a committee of five was created to revise and arrange the style of the articles agreed to by the Convention; and Johnson, Hamilton, Gouverneur Morris, Madison, and King were selected as members of this committee. Of these five men four, Hamilton, Morris, Madison and King, are on record as expressly favoring judicial control over legislation. There is some little dispute as to the share of glory to be assigned to single members of the committee, but undoubtedly Gouverneur Morris played a considerable part in giving to the Constitution its final form. Speaking of his work on the Constitution, Mr. Morris later wrote:

Having rejected redundant and equivocal terms, I believed it as clear as our language would permit; excepting, nevertheless, a part of what relates to the judiciary. On that subject conflicting opinions had been maintained with so much professional astuteness that it

---

[1] Farrand, vol. ii, p. 186.

became necessary to select phrases which expressing my own notions would not alarm others nor shock their self-love.[1]

That the Constitution was not designed to be perfectly explicit on all points and to embody definitely the opinions of the majority of the Convention is further evidenced by a speech made by Abraham Baldwin, a member of the Convention from Georgia, in the House of Representatives on March 14, 1796. In speaking of the clause of the Constitution which provides that treaties are to be the supreme law of the land, he said:

He would begin it by the assertion, that those few words in the Constitution on this subject were not those apt, precise, definite expressions, which irresistibly brought upon them the meaning which he had been above considering. He said it was not to disparage the instrument, to say that it had not definitely, and with precision, absolutely settled everything on which it had spoken. He had sufficient evidence to satisfy his own mind that it was not supposed by the makers of it at the time but that some subjects were left a little ambiguous and uncertain. It was a great thing to get so many difficult subjects definitely settled at once. If they could all be agreed in, it would compact the Government. The few that were left a little unsettled might, without any great risk, be settled by practice or by amendments in the progress of the Government. He believed this subject of the rival powers of legislation and treaty was one of them; the subject of the militia was another, and some question respecting the judiciary another. When he reflected on the immense difficulties and dangers of that trying occasion—the old Government prostrated, and a chance whether a new one could be agreed in—the recollection recalled to him nothing but the most joyful sensations that so many things had been so well settled, and that experience had shown there was very little difficulty or danger in settling the rest.[2]

---

[1] Sparks, *Life of Morris*, vol. iii, p. 323. Professor A. C. McLaughlin, in a letter to the author, suggests that the "conflicting opinions" referred to by Morris were not over the question of judicial review, but over the subjects of inferior federal courts and appeals from state tribunals.

[2] Farrand, vol. iii, p. 369.

3

Judicial Control Before the
Ratifying Conventions

It is urged by the opponents of judicial control that, whatever may have been the purpose of the members of the Philadelphia convention, the ratifying conventions in the states gave the final legal sanction to the Constitution, and a sound rule of interpretation would compel us to ascertain the opinion of these bodies on the point at issue. This contention cannot be gainsaid; but a full examination of the materials on the state conventions, as anyone can see, would require years of research into the lives and opinions of several hundred members. The author does not pretend to have made this research, and this essay is limited principally to a consideration of the purpose of the framers, not the enactors, of the Constitution. However, it is of interest to note what materials bearing on the purpose of the enactors with regard to this point are contained in Elliot's *Debates*.

If the members of the Virginia convention which ratified the federal Constitution were in the dark as to this matter, or had any doubts as to the probable implications of the judiciary article, they must have been enlightened by the clear and unmistakable language of John Marshall. In replying to objections which had been raised regarding the danger of an extension of federal jurisdiction at the cost of the states, he pointed out that the proposed federal government was one of enumerated and limited powers.

Has the government of the United States power to make laws on every subject? . . . Can they make laws affecting the mode of transferring property, or contracts, or claims between citizens of the same state? Can they go beyond the delegated powers? If they were to make a law not warranted by any of the powers enumerated it would be considered by the judges as an infringement of the Constitution which they are to guard. They would not consider such a law as coming under their jurisdiction. They would declare it void.[1]

In the course of the discussion, Mr. Grayson said: "If the Congress cannot make a law against the Constitution I apprehend they cannot make a law to abridge it. The judges are to defend it." [2] Mr. Pendleton declared: "The fair inference is that oppressive laws will not be warranted by the Constitution, nor attempted by our representatives, who are selected for their ability and integrity, and that honest, independent judges will never admit an oppressive construction." [3]

The Maryland convention was by no means uninformed regarding the possible functions of the judiciary under the proposed Constitution. In his famous letter directed to the legislature of the state, Luther Martin said:

Whether, therefore, any laws or regulations of the Congress or any acts of its president or other officers are contrary to, or not warranted by, the Constitution, rests only with the judges who are appointed by Congress to determine; by whose determinations every state must be bound.[4]

If the members of the Pennsylvania ratifying convention had any doubts regarding the probable exercise of judicial control over legislation under the new Constitution, these must have been removed by one of Mr. Wilson's speeches in defence of the judiciary. Some members of the convention expressed the apprehension that, inasmuch as the federal courts were to have jurisdiction in all cases

---

[1] Elliot's *Debates*, vol. iii, p. 553.
[2] *Ibid.*, p. 567.
[3] Elliot's *Debates*, vol. iii, p. 548.
[4] *Ibid.*, vol. i, p. 380.

in law and equity arising under the Constitution and the laws of the United States, the power enjoyed by the judges might be indefinitely extended if Congress saw fit to make laws not warranted by the Constitution. On this point Mr. Wilson said:

I think the contrary inference true. If a law should be made inconsistent with those powers vested by this instrument in Congress, the judges, as a consequence of their independence, and the particular powers of government being defined, will declare such law to be null and void. For the power of the Constitution predominates. Anything therefore that shall be enacted by Congress contrary thereto will not have the force of law.[1]

In New York, the members of the Convention must have known the clear and cogent argument for judicial control made by Hamilton in *The Federalist*.

If the members of the Connecticut convention were unaware of the fact that under the provisions of the Constitution the judiciary would enjoy the power to pass upon the constitutionality of federal and state statutes, it was their own fault; for, in his speech of January 7, 1788, on the power of Congress to lay taxes, Oliver Ellsworth carefully explained the new system. He said:

This constitution defines the extent of the powers of the general government. If the general legislature should at any time overleap their limits, the judicial department is a constitutional check. If the United States go beyond their powers, if they make a law which the Constitution does not authorize, it is void; and the judicial power, the national judges, who, to secure their impartiality, are to be made independent, will declare it to be void.[2]

It would be entirely misleading to conclude, from this fragmentary evidence, that the question of judicial control over acts of Congress was adequately considered in the state conventions. It was judicial control over state statutes that aroused the most serious apprehensions of critics of the new frame of government. That they thought much—or cared much—about what might hap-

---

[1] McMaster and Stone, *Pennsylvania and the Federal Constitution*, p. 354.
[2] Elliot's *Debates*, vol. ii, p. 196. *Cf.* Farrand, vol. iii, p. 240.

pen to acts of Congress is not apparent.[1] Still it cannot be said that they were kept in the dark in this respect, or that they could not easily have learned, if the matter had interested them, what the framers of the Constitution intended and expected. And it may pertinently be asked what our constitutional position would be to-day, if it were recognized that each branch of the federal government, in addition to the clearly expressed powers conferred upon it, possesses those additional powers only which were understood, by the ratifying conventions of the states, to have been impliedly conferred!

---

[1] It is interesting to note that when, ten years later, the Kentucky and Virginia Resolutions raised the question of judicial control, and the other states had occasion to express a direct opinion on this point, none of them seems to have approved the doctrine expressed in the Resolutions. *Cf.* Ames, *State Documents on Federal Relations*, p. 16. The Massachusetts legislature replied to Virginia, on February 9, 1799: "This legislature are persuaded that the decision of all cases in law and equity arising under the Constitution of the United States and the construction of all laws made in pursuance thereof are exclusively vested by the people in the judicial courts of the United States." *Ibid.*, pp. 18 *et seq.* The Rhode Island assembly declared that "the words, to wit, 'The judicial power shall extend to all cases arising under the laws of the United States,' vest in the federal courts exclusively, and in the Supreme Court of the United States ultimately, the authority of deciding on the constitutionality of any act or law of the Congress of the United States." *Ibid.*, p. 17. The New Hampshire legislature resolved: "That the state legislatures are not the proper tribunals to determine the constitutionality of the laws of the general government; that the duty of such decision is properly and exclusively confided to the judicial department." Elliot's *Debates*, vol. iv, p. 539 (ed. 1861). The Vermont legislature asserted: "It belongs not to state legislatures to decide on the constitutionality of laws made by the general government, this power being exclusively vested in the judiciary courts of the Union." *Ibid.* The House of Representatives of Pennsylvania replied to Kentucky that the people of the United States "have committed to the supreme judiciary of the nation the high authority of ultimately and conclusively deciding upon the constitutionality of all legislative acts." Ames, *op. cit.*, p. 420. The Senate of New York replied to Virginia and Kentucky that the decision of all cases in law and equity was confined to the federal judiciary and that the states were excluded from interference. *Ibid.*, p. 23.

4

The Spirit of the Constitution[1]

Those who hold that it was not the intention of the framers of the Constitution to establish judicial control of legislation make much of the opposition aroused by the sporadic attempts of a few state courts to exercise such a control prior to 1787. Dean Trickett cites the cases and exclaims: "These then are the precedents!" Mr. Boudin cites them and also exclaims: "Such were the state 'precedents,' and such was the temper of the people at the time the Philadelphia convention met to frame the Constitution of the United States." The only trouble with this line of argument is that it leaves out of account the sharp political division existing in the United States in 1787 and the following years.

The men who framed the federal Constitution were not among the paper-money advocates and stay-law makers whose operations in state legislatures and attacks upon the courts were chiefly responsible, Madison informs us, for the calling of the convention. The framers of the Constitution were not among those who favored the assaults on vested rights which legislative majorities were making throughout the Union. On the contrary, they were, almost without exception, bitter opponents of such enterprises; and they regarded it as their chief duty, in drafting the new Constitution, to find a

---

[1] In this chapter I have reprinted a few pages from my *American Government and Politics.*

way of preventing the renewal of what they deemed "legislative tyranny." Examine the rolls of the state conventions that ratified the Constitution after it came from the Philadelphia convention, and compare them with the rolls of the legislatures that had been assailing the rights of property. It was largely because the framers of the Constitution knew the temper and class bias of the state legislatures that they arranged that the new Constitution should be ratified by conventions.

The makers of the federal Constitution represented the solid, conservative, commercial and financial interests of the country —not the interests which denounced and proscribed judges in Rhode Island, New Jersey and North Carolina, and stoned their houses in New York. The conservative interests, made desperate by the imbecilities of the Confederation and harried by state legislatures, roused themselves from their lethargy, drew together in a mighty effort to establish a government that would be strong enough to pay the national debt, regulate interstate and foreign commerce, provide for national defence, prevent fluctuations in the currency created by paper emissions, and control the propensities of legislative majorities to attack private rights.

It is in the light of the political situation that existed in 1787 that we must inquire whether the principle of judicial control is out of harmony with the general purpose of the federal Constitution. It is an ancient and honorable rule of construction, laid down by Blackstone, that any instrument should be interpreted, "by considering the reason and spirit of it; or the cause which moved the legislator to enact it . . . From this method of interpreting laws, by the reason of them, arises what we call equity." It may be, therefore, that the issue of judicial control is a case in equity. The direct intention of the framers and enactors not being clearly expressed on this point, we may have recourse to the "reason and spirit" of the Constitution.

As Blackstone shows by happy illustration the reason and spirit of a law are to be understood only by an inquiry into the circumstances of its enactment. The underlying purposes of the Constitu-

THE SUPREME COURT AND THE CONSTITUTION

tion, therefore, are to be revealed only by a study of the conditions and events which led to its formation and adoption.

At the outset it must be remembered that there were two great parties at the time of the adoption of the Constitution—one laying emphasis on strength and efficiency in government and the other on its popular aspects. Quite naturally the men who led in stirring up the revolt against Great Britain and in keeping the fighting temper of the Revolutionists at the proper heat were the boldest and most radical thinkers—men like Samuel Adams, Thomas Paine, Patrick Henry, and Thomas Jefferson. They were not, generally speaking, men of large property interests or of much practical business experience. In a time of disorder, they could consistently lay more stress upon personal liberty than upon social control; and they pushed to the extreme limits those doctrines of individual rights which had been evolved in England during the struggles of the small landed proprietors and commercial classes against royal prerogative, and which corresponded to the economic conditions prevailing in America at the close of the eighteenth century. They associated strong government with monarchy, and came to believe that the best political system was one which governed least. A majority of the radicals viewed all government, especially if highly centralized, as a species of evil, tolerable only because necessary and always to be kept down to an irreducible minimum by a jealous vigilance.

Jefferson put the doctrine in concrete form when he declared that he preferred newspapers without government to government without newspapers. The Declaration of Independence, the first state Constitutions, and the Articles of Confederation bore the impress of this philosophy. In their anxiety to defend the individual against all federal interference and to preserve to the states a large sphere of local autonomy, these Revolutionists had set up a system too weak to accomplish the accepted objects of government; namely, national defence, the protection of property, and the advancement of commerce. They were not unaware of the character of their handiwork, but they believed with Jefferson that "man was a rational animal endowed by nature with rights and with an innate sense of justice and that he could be restrained from wrong and protected in right by moderate powers confided to persons of his own choice." Occasional riots and disorders, they held, were preferable to too much government.

The new American political system based on these doctrines had scarcely gone into effect before it began to incur opposition from many sources. The close of the Revolutionary struggle removed the prime cause for radical agitation and brought a new group of thinkers into prominence. When independence had been gained, the practical work to be done was the maintenance of social order, the payment of the public debt, the provision of a sound financial system, and the establishment of conditions favorable to the development of the economic resources of the new country. The men who were principally concerned in this work of peaceful enterprise were not the philosophers, but men of business and property and the holders of public securities. For the most part they had had no quarrel with the system of class rule and the strong centralization of government which existed in England. It was on the question of policy, not of governmental structure, that they had broken with the British authorities. By no means all of them, in fact, had even resisted the policy of the mother country, for within the ranks of the conservatives were large numbers of Loyalists who had remained in America, and, as was to have been expected, cherished a bitter feeling against the Revolutionists, especially the radical section which had been boldest in denouncing the English system root and branch. In other words, after the heat and excitement of the War of Independence were over and the new government, state and national, was tested by the ordinary experiences of traders, financiers, and manufacturers, it was found inadequate, and these groups accordingly grew more and more determined to reconstruct the political system in such a fashion as to make it subserve their permanent interests.

Under the state constitutions and the Articles of Confederation established during the Revolution, every powerful economic class in the nation suffered either immediate losses or from impediments placed in the way of the development of their enterprises. The holders of the securities of the Confederate government did not receive the interest on their loans. Those who owned western lands or looked with longing eyes upon the rich opportunities for speculation there, chafed at the weakness of the government and its delays in establishing order on the frontiers. Traders and commercial men found their plans for commerce on a national scale impeded by local interference with interstate commerce. The currency of the states and the nation was hopelessly muddled. Creditors everywhere were angry about the depreciated paper money which the agrarians had made and were attempting to force upon those from whom they had borrowed specie. In short, it was a war between business and populism. Under the Articles of Confederation populism had a free hand, for majorities in the state legislatures were omnipotent. Anyone who reads the economic history of the time will see why the solid conservative interests of the country were weary of talk about the "rights of the people" and bent upon establishing firm guarantees for the rights of property.

The Congress of the Confederation was not long in discovering the true character of the futile authority which the Articles had conferred upon it. The necessity for new sources of revenue became apparent even while the struggle for independnce was yet undecided, and, in 1781, Congress carried a resolution to the effect that it should be authorized to lay a duty of five per cent on certain goods. This moderate proposition was defeated because Rhode Island rejected it on the grounds that "she regarded it the most precious jewel of sovereignty that no state shall be called upon to open its purse but by the authority of the state and by her own officers." Two years later Congress prepared another amendment to the Articles providing for certain import duties, the receipts from which, collected by state officers, were to be applied to the payment of the public debt; but three years after the introduction of the measure, four states, including New York, still held out against its ratification, and the project was allowed to drop. At last, in 1786,

Congress in a resolution declared that the requisitions for the last eight years had been so irregular in their operation, so uncertain in their collection, and so evidently unproductive, that a reliance on them in the future would be no less dishonorable to the understandings of those who entertained it than it would be dangerous to the welfare and peace of the Union. Congress, thereupon, solemnly added that it had become its duty "to declare most explicitly that the crisis had arrived when the people of the United States, by whose will and for whose benefit the federal government was instituted, must decide whether they will support their rank as a nation by maintaining the public faith at home and abroad, or whether for the want of a timely exertion in establishing a general revenue and thereby giving strength to the Confederacy, they will hazard not only the existence of the Union but those great and invaluable privileges for which they have so arduously and so honorably contended."

In fact, the Articles of Confederation had hardly gone into effect before the leading citizens also began to feel that the powers of Congress were wholly inadequate. In 1780, even before their adoption, Alexander Hamilton proposed a general convention to frame a new constitution, and from that time forward he labored with remarkable zeal and wisdom to extend and popularize the idea of a strong national government. Two years later, the assembly of the state of New York recommended a convention to revise the Articles and increase the power of Congress. In 1783, Washington, in a circular letter to the governors, urged that it was indispensable to the happiness of the individual states that there should be lodged somewhere a supreme power to regulate and govern the general concerns of the confederation. Shortly afterward (1785), Governor Bowdoin, of Massachusetts, suggested to his state legislature the advisability of calling a national assembly to settle upon and define the powers of Congress; and the legislature resolved that the government under the Articles of Confederation was inadequate and should be reformed; but the resolution was never laid before Congress.

In January, 1786, Virginia invited all the other states to send delegates to a convention at Annapolis to consider the question of duties on imports and commerce in general. When this convention assembled in 1786, delegates from only five states were present, and they were disheartened at the limitations on their powers and the lack of interest the other states had shown in the project. With characteristic foresight, however, Alexander Hamilton seized the occasion to secure the adoption of a recommendation advising the states to choose representatives for another convention to meet in Philadelphia the following year "to consider the Articles of Confederation and to propose such changes therein as might render them adequate to the exigencies of the union." This recommendation was cautiously worded, for Hamilton did not want to raise any unnecessary alarm. He doubtless believed that a complete revolution in the old system was desirable, but he knew that, in the existing state of popular temper, it was not expedient to announce his complete program. Accordingly no general reconstruction of the political system was suggested; the Articles of Confederation were merely to be "revised"; and the amendments were to be approved by the state legislatures as provided by that instrument.

The proposal of the Annapolis convention was transmitted to the state legislatures and laid before Congress. Congress thereupon resolved in February, 1787, that a convention should be held for the sole and express purpose of revising the Articles of Confederation and reporting to itself and the legislatures of the several states such alterations and provisions as would when agreed to by Congress and confirmed by the states render the federal constitution adequate to the exigencies of government and the preservation of the union.

In pursuance of this call, delegates to the new convention were chosen by the legislatures of the states or by the governors in conformity to authority conferred by the legislative assemblies.[1] The

---

[1] Rhode Island alone was unrepresented. In all sixty-two delegates were appointed by the states; fifty-five of these attended sometime during the sessions; but only thirty-nine signed the finished document.

delegates were given instructions of a general nature by their respective states, none of which, apparently, contemplated any very far-reaching changes. In fact, almost all of them expressly limited their representatives to a mere revision of the Articles of Confederation. For example, Connecticut authorized her delegates to represent and confer for the purpose mentioned in the resolution of Congress and to discuss such measures "agreeably to the general principles of Republican government" as they should think proper to render the Union adequate. Delaware, however, went so far as to provide that none of the proposed alterations should extend to the fifth part of the Articles of Confederation guaranteeing that each state should be entitled to one vote.

It was a truly remarkable assembly of men that gathered in Philadelphia on May 14, 1787, to undertake the work of reconstructing the American system of government. It is not merely patriotic pride that compels one to assert that never in the history of assemblies has there been a convention of men richer in political experience and in practical knowledge, or endowed with a profounder insight into the springs of human action and the intimate essence of government. It is indeed an astounding fact that at one time so many men skilled in statecraft could be found on the very frontiers of civilization among a population numbering about four million whites. It is no less a cause for admiration that their instrument of government should have survived the trials and crises of a century that saw the wreck of more than a score of paper constitutions.

All the members had had a practical training in politics. Washington, as commander-in-chief of the revolutionary forces, had learned well the lessons and problems of war, and mastered successfully the no less difficult problems of administration. The two Morrises had distinguished themselves in grappling with financial questions as trying and perplexing as any which statesmen had ever been compelled to face. Seven of the delegates had gained political wisdom as governors of their native states; and no less than twenty-eight had served in Congress either during the Revolution or under the Articles of Confederation. There were men trained in the law, versed in finance, skilled in administration, and learned in the political philosophy of their own and all earlier times. Moreover, they were men destined to continue public service under the government which they had met to construct—Presidents, Vice-Presidents, heads of departments, justices of the Supreme Court were in that imposing body. They were equal to the great task of constructing a national system strong enough to defend the country on land and sea, pay every dollar of the lawful debt, and afford sufficient guarantees to the rights of private property. The radicals, however, like Patrick Henry, Jefferson, and Samuel Adams, were conspicuous by their absence from the convention.

As Woodrow Wilson has concisely put it, the framers of the Constitution represented "a strong and intelligent class possessed of unity and informed by a conscious solidarity of interests." [1] They were not convened to write a Declaration of Independence, but to frame a government which would meet the practical issues that had arisen under the Articles of Confederation. The objections they entertained to direct popular government, and they were undoubtedly many, were based upon their experience with popular assemblies during the immediately preceding years. With many of the plain lessons of history before them, they naturally feared that the rights and privileges of the minority would be insecure if the principle of majority rule was definitely adopted and provisions made for its exercise. Furthermore, it will be remembered that up to that time the right of all men, as men, to share in the government had never been recognized in practice. Everywhere in Europe the government was in the hands of a ruling monarch or at best a ruling class; everywhere the mass of the people had been regarded principally as an arms-bearing and tax-paying multitude, uneducated, and with little hope or capacity for advancement. Two years were to elapse after the meeting of the grave assembly at Philadelphia before the transformation of the Estates General into

---

[1] *Division and Reunion*, p. 12.

the National Convention in France opened the floodgates of revolutionary ideas on human rights before whose rising tide old landmarks of government are still being submerged. It is small wonder, therefore, that under the circumstances, many of the members of that august body held popular government in slight esteem and took the people into consideration only as far as it was imperative "to inspire them with the necessary confidence," as Mr. Gerry frankly put it.[1]

Indeed, every page of the laconic record of the proceedings of the convention preserved to posterity by Mr. Madison shows conclusively that the members of that assembly were not seeking to realize any fine notions about democracy and equality, but were striving with all the resources of political wisdom at their command to set up a system of government that would be stable and efficient, safeguarded on one hand against the possibilities of despotism and on the other against the onslaught of majorities. In the mind of Mr. Gerry, the evils they had experienced flowed "from the excess of democracy," and he confessed that while he was still republican, he "had been taught by experience the danger of the levelling spirit." [2] Mr. Randolph in offering to the consideration of the convention his plan of government, observed "that the general object was to provide a cure for the evils under which the United States labored; that, in tracing these evils to their origin, every man had found it in the turbulence and follies of democracy; that some check therefore was to be sought for against this tendency of our governments; and that a good Senate seemed most likely to answer the purpose." [3] Mr. Hamilton, in advocating a life term for Senators, urged that "all communities divide themselves into the few and the many. The first are rich and well born and the other the mass of the people who seldom judge or determine right."

Gouverneur Morris wanted to check the "precipitancy, changeableness, and excess" of the representatives of the people by the

---

[1] Elliot's *Debates,* vol. v, p. 160.

[2] *Ibid.,* vol. v, p. 136.

[3] Elliot's *Debates*, vol. v, p. 138.

ability and virtue of men "of great and established property—aristocracy; men who from pride will support consistency and permanency . . . Such an aristocratic body will keep down the turbulence of democracy." While these extreme doctrines were somewhat counter-balanced by the democratic principles of Mr. Wilson who urged that "the government ought to possess, not only first, the force, but second the mind or sense of the people at large," Madison doubtless summed up in a brief sentence the general opinion of the convention when he said that to secure private rights against majority factions, and at the same time to preserve the spirit and form of popular government, was the great object to which their inquiries had been directed.[1]

They were anxious above everything else to safeguard the rights of private property against any levelling tendencies on the part of the propertyless masses. Gouverneur Morris, in speaking on the problem of apportioning representatives, correctly stated the sound historical fact when he declared: "Life and liberty were generally said to be of more value than property. An accurate view of the matter would, nevertheless, prove that property was the main object of society . . . If property, then, was the main object of government, certainly it ought to be one measure of the influence due to those who were to be affected by the government." [2] Mr. King also agreed that "property was the primary object of society;" [3] and Mr. Madison warned the convention that in framing a system which they wished to last for ages they must not lose sight of the changes which the ages would produce in the forms and distribution of property. In advocating a long term in order to give independence and firmness to the Senate, he described these impending changes: "An increase of population will of necessity increase the proportion of those who will labor under all the hardships of life and secretly sigh for a more equal distribution of its blessings. These may in time outnumber those who are placed above the feelings

---

[1] *The Federalist,* No. 10.

[2] Elliot's *Debates,* vol. v, p. 279.

[3] *Ibid.,* vol. v, p. 280.

of indigence. According to the equal laws of suffrage, the power will slide into the hands of the former. No agrarian attempts have yet been made in this country, but symptoms of a levelling spirit, as we have understood have sufficiently appeared, in a certain quarter, to give notice of the future danger." [1] And again, in support of the argument for a property qualification on voters, Madison urged, "In future times, a great majority of the people will not only be without landed, but any other sort of property. These will either combine, under the influence of their common situation,—in which case the rights of property and the public liberty will not be secure in their hands,—or, what is more probable, they will become the tools of opulence and ambition; in which case there will be equal danger on another side." [2] Various projects for setting up class rule by the establishment of property qualifications for voters and officers were advanced in the convention, but they were defeated. On account of the diversity of opinion that prevailed, agreement was impossible, and it was thought best to trust this matter to the discretion and wisdom of the states.

Nevertheless, by the system of checks and balances placed in the government, the convention safeguarded the interests of property against attacks by majorities. The House of Representatives, Mr. Hamilton pointed out, "was so formed as to render it particularly the guardian of the poorer orders of citizens," [3] while the Senate was to preserve the rights of property and the interests of the minority against the demands of the majority.[4] In the tenth number of *The Federalist*, Mr. Madison argued in a philosophic vein in support of the proposition that it was necessary to base the political system on the actual conditions of "natural inequality." Uniformity of interests throughout the state, he contended, was impossible on account of the diversity in the faculties of men, from which the rights of property originated; the protection of these

---

[1] Elliot's *Debates*, vol. v, p. 243.

[2] *Ibid.*, vol. v, p. 387.

[3] Elliot's *Debates*, vol. v, p. 244.

[4] *Ibid.*, vol. v, p. 203.

faculties was the first object of government; from the protection of different and unequal faculties of acquiring property the possession of different degrees and kinds of property immediately resulted; from the influence of these on the sentiments and views of the respective proprietors ensued a division of society into different interests and parties; the unequal distribution of wealth inevitably led to a clash of interests in which the majority was liable to carry out its policies at the expense of the minority; hence, he added in concluding this splendid piece of logic "the majority, having such coexistent passion or interest, must be rendered by their number and local situation unable to concert and carry into effect schemes of oppression"; and in his opinion it was the great merit of the newly framed Constitution that it secured the rights of the minority against "the superior force of an interested and overbearing majority."

This very system of checks and balances, which is undeniably the essential element of the Constitution, is built upon the doctrine that the popular branch of the government cannot be allowed full sway, and least of all in the enactment of laws touching the rights of property. The exclusion of the direct popular vote in the election of the President; the creation, again by indirect election, of a Senate which the framers hoped would represent the wealth and conservative interests of the country; and the establishment of an independent judiciary appointed by the President with the concurrence of the Senate—all these devices bear witness to the fact that the underlying purpose of the Constitution was not the establishment of popular government by means of parliamentary majorities.

Page after page of *The Federalist* is directed to that portion of the electorate which was disgusted with the "mutability of the public councils." Writing on the presidential veto Hamilton says:

The propensity of the legislative department to intrude upon the rights, and absorb the powers, of the other departments has already been suggested and repeated. . . . It may perhaps be said that the power of preventing bad laws included the power of preventing good ones; and may be used to the one purpose as well as the other. But this objection will have little weight with those who can properly estimate the mischiefs of that inconstancy and mutability in the laws which form the greatest blemish in the character and genius of our governments. They will consider every institution calculated to restrain the excess of law-making and to keep things in the same state in which they happen to be at any given period, as more likely to do good than harm; because it is favorable to greater stability in the system of legislation. The injury which may be possibly done by defeating a few good laws will be amply compensated by the advantage of preventing a number of bad ones.

When the framers of the Constitution had completed the remarkable instrument which was to establish a national government capable of discharging effectively certain great functions and checking the propensities of popular legislatures to attack the rights of private property, a formidable task remained before them—the task of securing the adoption of the new frame of government by states torn with popular dissensions. They knew very well that the state legislatures which had been so negligent in paying their quotas under the Articles and which had been so jealous of their rights, would probably stick at ratifying such a national instrument of government. Accordingly they cast aside that clause in the Articles requiring amendments to be ratified by the legislatures of all the states; and advised that the new Constitution should be ratified by conventions in the several states composed of delegates chosen by the voters. They furthermore declared—and this is a fundamental matter—that when the conventions of nine states had ratified the Constitution the new government should go into effect so far as those states were concerned. The chief reason for resorting to ratifications by conventions is laid down by Hamilton in the twenty-second number of *The Federalist*: "It has not a little contributed to the infirmities of the existing federal system that it never had a ratification by the people. Resting on no better foundation than the consent of the several legislatures, it has been exposed to frequent and intricate questions concerning the validity of its powers; and has in some instances given birth to the enormous doctrine of a right of legislative repeal. Owing its ratification to the law of a state, it has been contended that the same authority might repeal the law by which it was ratified. However gross a heresy it may be to maintain that a party to a compact has a right to revoke that compact, the doctrine itself has respectable advocates. The possibility of a question of this nature proves the necessity of laying the foundations of our national government deeper than in the mere sanction of delegated authority. The fabric of American empire ought to rest on the solid basis of the consent of the people. The streams of national power ought to flow immediately from that pure original fountain of all legitimate authority."

Of course, the convention did not resort to the revolutionary policy of transmitting the Constitution directly to the conventions of the several states. It merely laid the finished instrument before the Confederate Congress with the suggestion that it should be submitted to "a convention of delegates chosen in each state by the people thereof, under the recommendation of its legislature, for their assent and ratification; and each convention assenting thereto and ratifying the same should give notice thereof to the United States in Congress assembled." The convention went on to suggest that when nine states had ratified the Constitution, the Confederate Congress should extinguish itself by making provision for the elections necessary to put the new government into effect. "What they [the convention] actually did, stripped of all fiction and verbiage," says Professor Burgess, "was to assume constituent powers, ordain a Constitution of government and of liberty, and demand the *plébiscite* thereon, over the heads of all existing legally organized powers. Had Julius or Napoleon committed these acts, they would have been pronounced *coups d'état.* Looked at from the side of the people exercising the *plébiscite,* we term the movement revolution. The convention clothed its acts and assumptions in more moderate language than I have used, and professed to follow a more legal course than I have indicated. The exact form of procedure was as follows: They placed in the body of the proposed

Constitution itself a provision declaring that ratifications by conventions of the people in nine states (commonwealths) should be
sufficient for the establishment of the Constitution between the
states (commonwealths) so ratifying the same. They then sent the
instrument entire to the Confederate Congress, with the direction,
couched in terms of advice, that the Congress should pass it along,
untouched, to the legislatures of the commonwealths, and that these
should pass it along, also untouched, to conventions of the people
in each commonwealth, and that when nine conventions should
have approved, Congress should take steps to put the new government into operation and abdicate. Of course the mass of the
people were not at all able to analyze the real character of this
procedure. It is probable that many of the members of the convention itself did not fully comprehend just what they were doing.
Not many of them had had sufficient education as publicists to be
able to generalize the scientific import of their acts." [1]

After the new Constitution was published and transmitted to
the states, there began a long and bitter fight over ratification. A
veritable flood of pamphlet literature descended upon the country,
and a collection of these pamphlets by Hamilton, Madison, and
Jay, brought together under the title of *The Federalist*—though
clearly a piece of campaign literature—has remained a permanent
part of the contemporary sources on the Constitution and has been
regarded by many lawyers as a commentary second in value only
to the decisions of the Supreme Court. Within a year the champions
of the new government found themselves victorious, for on June
21, 1788, the ninth state, New Hampshire, ratified the Constitution, and accordingly the new government might go into effect as
between the agreeing states. Within a few weeks, the nationalist
party in Virginia and New York succeeded in winning these two
states, and in spite of the fact that North Carolina and Rhode Island
had not yet ratified the Constitution, Congress determined to put

---

[1] Burgess, *Political Science and Constitutional Law,* vol. i, p. 105.

the instrument into effect in accordance with the recommendations of the convention. Elections for the new government were held; the date March 4, 1789, was fixed for the formal establishment of the new system; Congress secured a quorum on April 6; and on April 30 Washington was inaugurated at the Federal Hall in Wall Street, New York.

5

The Supporters of the New Constitution

The new Constitution was ratified by conventions of delegates chosen at the polls; but it should be remembered that, under the property qualifications then imposed upon the suffrage, a large proportion of the adult males were debarred from participating in the elections. Generally speaking, the propertyless, who were disgruntled with the handiwork of the Philadelphia conference, could do nothing but gnash their teeth.

Among those who led in the ratification of the new Constitution everywhere were men of substantial property interests who had suffered most from the enterprises of the state legislatures. The supporters of the new instrument in the states included in their ranks the leaders in every economic activity: merchants, traders, shippers, land dealers, lawyers, capitalists, financiers, and professional men. This fact is conclusively demonstrated by Dr. Libby's study[1] of the ratification of the Constitution and it is illustrated by the following letters and papers written by keen observers during the period of the struggle over the adoption of the new system of government.

William Grayson to James Monroe.

New York, May 29, 1787.

The delegates [to the Philadelphia convention] from the Eastward are for a very strong government, and wish to prostrate all

---

[1] *Geographical Distribution of the Vote of the Thirteen States on the Federal Constitution.* Wisconsin University Publications (1897).

the state legislatures, and form a general system out of the whole; but I don't learn that the people are with them, on the contrary in Massachusetts they think that government too strong and are about rebelling again, for the purpose of making it more demo-cratical: In Connecticut they have rejected the requisition for the present year decidedly, and no man there would be elected to the office of a constable if he was to declare that he meant to pay a copper towards the domestic debt:—Rhode Island has refused to send members—the cry there is for a good government after they have paid their debts in depreciated paper:—first demolish the Philistines, *i.e.* their creditors, and then for *propriety.*

New Hampshire has not paid a shilling, since peace, and does not ever mean to pay one to all eternity:—if it was attempted to tax the people for the domestic debt 500 Shays would arise in a fortnight.—In New York they pay well because they do it by plundering New Jersey and Connecticut.—Jersey will go great lengths from motives of revenge and Interest: Pennsylvania will join provided you let the sessions of the Executive of America be fixed in Philadelphia and give her other advantages in trade to compen-sate for the loss of state power. I shall make no observations on the southern states, but I think they will be, perhaps from different motives, as little disposed to part with efficient power as any in the Union.[1]

D. Humphreys to George Washington.
New Haven, Sept. 28, 1787.
All the different classes in the liberal professions will be in favour of the proposed Constitution. The clergy, lawyers, physicians and merchants will have considerable influence on society. Nor will the officers of the late army be backward in expressing their approba-tion. Indeed the well affected have not been wanting in efforts to prepare the minds of the citizens for the favorable reception of whatever might be the result of your proceedings. I have had no inconsiderable agency in the superintendence of two presses, from which more newspapers are circulated, I imagine, than from any others in New England. Judicious and well-timed publications have great efficacy in ripening the judgment of men in this quarter of the continent.[2]

---

[1] *Documentary History of the Constitution,* vol. i, pp. 170-171.
[2] *Ibid.,* vol. i, p. 302.

Conjectures about the New Constitution by Hamilton, Autumn, 1787.

The new Constitution has in favor of its success these circumstances—a very great weight of influence of the persons who framed it, particularly in the universal popularity of General Washington— the good will of the commercial interest throughout the states which will give all its efforts to the establishment of a government capable of regulating, protecting and extending the commerce of the Union—The good will of most men of property in the several states who wish a government of the union able to protect them against domestic violence and the depradations which the democratic spirit is apt to make on property;—and who are besides anxious for the respectability of the nation—a strong belief in the people at large of the insufficiency of the present confederation to preserve the existence of the union and of the necessity of the union to their safety and prosperity; of course a strong desire of a change and a predisposition to receive well the propositions of the convention.

Against the success is to be put the influence of many *inconsiderable* men in possession of considerable offices under the state governments who will fear a diminution of their consequence, power and emolument by the establishment of the general government and who can hope for nothing there—the influence of some *considerable* men in office possessed of talents and popularity who partly from the same motives and partly from a desire of *playing a part* in a convulsion for their own aggrandisement will oppose the quiet adoption of the new government—(some considerable men out of office, from motives of ambition may be disposed to act the same part)—add to these causes the democratical jealousy of the people which may be alarmed at the appearance of institutions that may seem calculated to place the power of the community in few hands and to raise a few individuals to stations of great preëminence— and the influence of some foreign powers who from different motives will not wish to see an energetic government established throughout the states.[1]

James Madison to Thomas Jefferson.

December 9, 1787.

It is worthy of remark that whilst in Virginia and some of the other states in the middle and southern districts of the Union, the

---

[1] *Documentary History of the Constitution,* vol. i, pp. 288-289.

men of intelligence, patriotism, property, and independent circumstances, are thus divided; all of this description, with a few exceptions, in the eastern states, and most of the middle states, are zealously attached to the proposed Constitution. In New England, the men of letters, the principal officers of Govt., the judges and lawyers, the clergy, and men of property, furnish only here and there an adversary. It is not less worthy of remark that in Virginia where the mass of the people have been so much accustomed to be guided by their rulers on all new and intricate questions, they should on the present which certainly surpasses the judgment of the greater part of them, not only go before, but contrary to, their most popular leaders. And the phenomenon is the more wonderful, as a popular ground is taken by all the adversaries to the new Constitution. Perhaps the solution in both these cases, would not be very difficult; but it would lead to observations too diffusive; and to you unnecessary. I will barely observe that the case in Virga. seems to prove that the body of sober and steady people, even of the lower order, are tired of the vicissitudes, injustice and follies which have so much characterised public measures, and are impatient for some change which promises stability and repose.[1]

H. Knox to Gen Washington.

New York, Jan. 14, 1788.

Colonel Wadsworth writes me that the present Governor and Lieutenant Governor, the late Governor, the judges of the Supreme Court and the Council were of the convention and all for the constitution excepting Jas. Wadsworth.

The Massachusetts convention were to meet on the 9th. The decision of Connecticut will influence in a degree their determination and I have no doubt that the Constitution will be adopted in Massachusetts.—But it is at this moment questionable whether it will be by a large majority.

There are three parties existing in that state at present, differing in their numbers and greatly differing in their wealth and talents.

The 1st is the commercial part, of the state to which are added, all the men of considerable property, the clergy, the lawyers— including all the judges of all the courts, and all the officers of the late army, and also the neighbourhood of all the great towns—its numbers may include ¾ths of the state. This party are for the most vigorous government, perhaps many of them would have been still

---

[1] *Ibid.*, vol. i, p. 398.

more pleased with the new Constitution had it been more analogous to the British Constitution.

The 2d party, are the eastern part of the state lying beyond New Hampshire formerly the Province of Main—This party are chiefly looking towards the erection of a new state, and the majority of them will adopt or reject the new Constitution as it may facilitate or retard their designs, without regarding the merits of the great question—this party $\frac{2}{7}$ ths.

The 3d party are the Insurgents, or their favorers, the great majority of whom are for an annihilation of debts, public and private, and therefore they will not approve the new Constitution—this party $\frac{2}{7}$ ths.

If the 1st and 2d party agree as will be most probable, and also some of the party stated as in the insurgent interest, the Constitution will be adopted by a great majority notwithstanding all the exertions to the contrary[1]

In letters written by Rufus King to Madison dated in January, 1788, he said:

Our convention [in Massachusetts] proceeds slowly; and apprehension that the liberties of the people are in danger, and a distrust of men of property or education have a more powerful effect upon the minds of our opponents than any specific objections against the Constitution. . . . The friends of the Constitution, who in addition to their own weight are respectable as they represent a very large proportion of the good sense and property of this state, have the task not only of answering, but also of stating and bringing forward the objections of their opponents. The opposition complains that the lawyers, judges, clergymen, merchants and men of education are all in favor of the Constitution—and that for that reason they appear to be able to make the worse appear the better cause. But say they, if we had men of this description on our side, we should alarm the people with the imperfections of the Constitution and be able to refute the defence set up in its favor. Notwithstanding the superiority of talent in favor of the Constitution, yet the same infatuation which prevailed not many months since in several counties of this state, and which emboldened them to take arms against the government, seems to have an uncontrollable authority over a numerous part of the convention. These objections

---

[1] *Documentary History of the Constitution,* vol. i, p. 442.

are not directed against any part of the Constitution, but their opposition seems to arise from an opinion that is immovable, that some injury is plotted against them—that the system is the production of the rich and ambitious, that they discover its operations and that the consequence will be the establishment of two orders in the Society, one comprehending the opulent and great, the other the poor and illiterate. The extraordinary Union in favor of the Constitution in this state of the wealthy and sensible part of it, is in confirmation of these opinions and every exertion hitherto made to eradicate it, has been in vain.[1]

Jabez Bowen to George Washington.

Providence, Dec. 15, 1789.

The towns of Newport, Providence, Bristol, etc., with the whole mercantile interest in the other towns in the state are federal, while the farmers in general are against it. Their opposition arises principally from their being much in debt, from the insinuations of wicked and designing men, that they will lose their liberty by adopting it; that the salaries of the national officers are so verry high that it will take the whole of the money collected by the impost to pay them, that the intrest and principal of the general debt must be raised by dry taxation on real estates, etc. We have exerted our utmost abilities to convince them of the errors that they have imbibed by hearing to the *old Tories* and *desperate debtors,* but all in vain, what further, sir, is to be done? if we knew what our duty was, we are willing to do it, tho' I have no idea that the Antis will or can be induced to come in without the arm of power is exerted and that they shall be taught that the principles that they hould and Disseminate among the citizens of the neighboring states as well as this is inconsistent, and not proper to be professed by any person or persons that live on the territories of the United States: their wish is to overturn the whole Federal Government rather than this state should submit to it. If we fail in getting a convention at the next meeting of the general assembly, will Congress *protect* us if we separate from the State Government and appoint us officers to collect the revenue; if this should be thought well of and should be put in practice but in part I have no doubt but it will bring the country part of the community to their senses soon—and that one town and another will be a dropping off so that the opposition will

---

[1] Rufus King. *Life and Letters,* vol. i, pp. 314, 316.

be done away. Be pleased, sir, to give me an answer to this proposition as soon as convenient.[1]

On reading these papers by representative and thoughtful men of the period, it is difficult to escape the conclusion that the Constitution was looked upon as a bulwark against populism of every form. Surely men of the type here quoted as in support of the new instrument of government must have rejoiced in the knowledge (spread abroad by *The Federalist)* that an independent judiciary was to guard the personal and property rights of minorities against all legislatures, state and national.

Indeed, it would seem to be a work of supererogation to argue such a proposition, were it not for the misleading notions about the American political system which are all too current. Every serious student of the history of our public law and policy has known that the defence of the rights of minorities against majorities is one of the fundamental purposes of our system of government. "I have thought," said Mr. Choate in his moving argument in the Income Tax Cases before the Supreme Court, "that one of the fundamental objects of all civilized government was the preservation of the rights of private property. I have thought that it was the very keystone of the arch upon which all civilized government rests, and that this once abandoned, everything was at stake and danger. . . . If it be true, as my friend said in closing, that the passions of the people are aroused on this subject, if it be true that a mighty army of sixty millions is likely to be incensed by this decision, it is the more vital to the future welfare of this country that this court again resolutely and courageously declare, as Marshall did, that it has the power to set aside an act of Congress violative of the Constitution, and that it will not hesitate in executing that power, no matter what the threatened consequences of popular or populistic wrath may be."

---

[1] *Documentary History of the Constitution,* vol. ii, p. 226.

6

John Marshall and the Fathers

The great Justice who made the theory of judicial control operative had better opportunities than any student of history or law to-day to discover the intention of the framers of the federal Constitution. Marshall, to be sure, did not have before him Elliot's *Debates*, but he was of the generation that made the Constitution. He had been a soldier in the Revolutionary War. He had been a member of the Virginia convention that ratified the Constitution; and he must have remembered stating in that convention the doctrine of judicial control,[1] apparently without arousing any protest. He was on intimate, if not always friendly, relations with the great men of his state who were instrumental in farming the Constitution. Washington once offered him the attorney-generalship. He was an envoy to France with two members of the convention, Charles Cotesworth Pinckney and Elbridge Gerry. He was a member of Congress for part of one term in Adams's administration; he was secretary of state under Adams; and he was everywhere regarded as a tower of strength to the Federalists.

---

[1] *Cf. supra*, p. 69. In his argument in the case of Ware *v.* Hylton before the Supreme Court in 1796, Marshall said: "The legislative authority of any country can only be restrained by its own municipal constitution. This is a principle that springs from the very nature of society; and the judicial authority can have no right to question the validity of a law unless such a jurisdiction is expressly given by the Constitution." 3 Dallas, 211. Here, however, Marshall was arguing as counsel, not stating his own personal views.

As Marshall's colleague, Story, has truly said of him:

He became enamored, not of a wild and visionary Republic, found only in the imaginations of mere enthusiasts as to human perfection, or tricked out in false colors by the selfish to flatter the prejudices or cheat the vanity of the people; but of that well-balanced Republic, adapted to human wants and human infirmities, in which power is to be held in check by countervailing power; and life, liberty and property are to be secured by a real and substantial independence, as well as division of the Legislative, Executive, and Judicial departments. . . . He was in the original, genuine sense of the word, a Federalist—a Federalist of the good old school, of which Washington was the acknowledged head, and in which he lived and died. In the maintenance of the principles of that school he was ready at all times to stand forth a determined advocate and supporter. On this subject he scorned all disguise; he affected no change of opinion; he sought no shelter from reproach.

It was, therefore, no closet philosopher, ignorant of the conditions under which the Constitution was established and unlearned in the reason and spirit of that instrument, who first enunciated from the supreme bench in unmistakable language the doctrine that judicial control over legislation was implied in the provisions of the federal Constitution.[1]

Those who hold that the framers of the Constitution did not intend to establish judicial control over federal legislation sometimes assert that Marshall made the doctrine out of whole cloth and had no precedents or authority to guide him. This is misleading. It is true that it was Marshall who first formally declared an act of Congress unconstitutional; but the fact should not be

---

[1] It has not escaped close observers, that the law which Marshall declared unconstitutional in Marbury v. Madison was a part of the Judiciary Act of 1789, which had been drafted and carried through by men who had served in the Convention. An analysis of the decision shows, however, that the section set aside was at most badly drawn and was not in direct conflict with the Constitution. Had Marshall been so inclined he might have construed the language of the act in such a manner as to have escaped the necessity of declaring it unconstitutional. *The Nation*, vol. lxxii, p. 104. The opportunity for asserting the doctrine, however, was too good to be lost, and Marshall was astute enough to take advantage of it. In view of the recent Jeffersonian triumph, he might very well have felt the need of having the great precedent firmly set.

overlooked that in the case of Hylton *v.* the United States[1] the Supreme Court, with Ellsworth[2] as Chief Justice and Paterson was Associate Justice (both members of the convention), exercised the right to pass upon the constitutionality of an act of Congress imposing a duty on carriages. On behalf of the appellant in this case it was argued that the law was unconstitutional and void in so far as it imposed a direct tax without apportionment among the states. The Court sustained the statute. If it was not understood that the Court had the power to hold acts of Congress void on constitutional grounds, why was the case carried before it? If the Court believed that it did not have the power to declare the act void as well as the power to sustain it, why did it assume jurisdiction at all or take the trouble to consider and render an opinion on the constitutionality of the tax?

The doctrine of judicial control was a familiar one in legal circles throughout the period between the formation of the Constitution and the year 1803, when Marshall decided the Marbury case. In Hayburn's case, already cited, the federal judges had refused to execute a statute which they held to be unconstitutional. This was in 1792. In 1794, in the case of Glass *v.* The Sloop Betsey,[3] the Supreme Court heard the doctrine of judicial control laid down by the counsel of the appellants:

The well-being of the whole depends upon keeping each department within its limits. In the state governments several instances have occurred where a legislative act has been rendered inoperative by a judicial decision that it was unconstitutional; and even under the federal government the judges, for the same reason, have refused to execute an act of Congress. . . . To the judicial and not to the executive department, the citizen or subject naturally looks for determinations upon his property; and that agreeably to known rules and settled forms to which no other security is equal.

---

[1] 3 Dallas, 171 (1796).

[2] Ellsworth did not take part in the decision, for he had just been sworn into office.

[3] 3 Dallas, 13.

In the case of Calder *v.* Bull,[1] decided in 1798, the counsel for the plaintiffs in error argued "that any law of the federal government or of any of the state governments contrary to the Constitution of the United States is void; and that this court possesses the power to declare such law void." Justice Chase however refused to pass upon the general principle, because it was not necessary to the decision of the case before him. He said:

Without giving an opinion at this time whether this court has jurisdiction to decide that any law made by Congress is void, I am fully satisfied that this court has no jurisdiction to determine that any law of any state legislature contrary to the constitution of such state is void.[2]

In the same case Justice Iredell said:

If any act of Congress or of the legislature of a state violates those constitutional provisions, it is unquestionably void; though I admit, that as the authority to declare it void is of a delicate and awful nature, the court will never resort to that authority but in a clear and urgent case.

In view of the principles entertained by the leading members of the convention with whom Marshall was acquainted, in view of the doctrine so clearly laid down in number 78 of *The Federalist,* in view of the arguments made more than once by eminent counsel before the Supreme Court, in view of Hayburn's case and Hylton *v.* the United States, in view of the judicial opinions several times expressed, in view of the purpose and spirit of the federal Constitution, it is difficult to understand the temerity of those who speak of the power asserted by Marshall in Marbury *v.* Madison as "usurpation."

---

[1] 3 Dallas, 386.

[2] Of course, as everybody knows, Chase adhered stoutly to the doctrine of federal judicial control.

7

Marbury *v.* Madison[1]

In this celebrated case decided in 1803, Chief Justice Marshall definitely applied for the first time in the name of the Supreme Court the principle that the federal judiciary enjoyed the power of passing upon the constitutionality of the acts of Congress. The case grew out of an application by Marbury to the Supreme Court for a mandamus compelling the Secretary of State, Madison, to deliver to him a commission as justice of the peace in the District of Columbia—an office to which he had been appointed in the closing days of the Adams administration. On his accession to power, Mr. Jefferson, specially embittered by the unseemly haste of the Federalists to engross as many officers as possible, refused to deliver to Marbury his commission. In the first part of his opinion, Chief Justice Marshall discussed the questions as to whether Marbury was duly entitled to his commission, and whether mandamus was the remedy. On these two points he came to affirmative conclusions, but the application for mandamus was denied on the ground that the authority given to the Supreme Court, by the Judiciary Act, to issue a writ of mandamus in such a case was not warranted by the Constitution. The general principles on which Chief Justice Marshall rested his argument are laid down in the following extracts from his opinion in the case.

---

[1] Cranch, 137.

By comparing them with the doctrines already enunciated by Hamilton, Paterson, and other leaders in the convention, one can see how closely Marshall caught the spirit of the Constitution.

The authority, therefore, given to the Supreme Court, by the act establishing the judicial courts of the United States, to issue writs of mandamus to public officers appears not to be warranted by the Constitution; and it becomes necessary to inquire whether a jurisdiction so conferred can be exercised.

The question whether an act repugnant to the Constitution can become the law of the land, is a question deeply interesting to the United States; but, happily, not of an intricacy proportioned to its interest. It seems only necessary to recognize certain principles, supposed to have been long and well established, to decide it.

That the people have an original right to establish, for their future government, such principles as, in their opinion, shall most conduce to their own happiness, is the basis on which the whole American fabric has been erected. The exercise of this original right is a very great exertion; nor can it, nor ought it to be frequently repeated. The principles, therefore, so established, are deemed fundamental. And as the authority from which they proceed is supreme, and can seldom act, they are designed to be permanent.

This original and supreme will organizes the government, and assigns to different departments their respective powers. It may either stop here, or establish certain limits not to be transcended by those departments.

The government of the United States is of the latter description. The powers of the legislature are defined and limited; and that those limits may not be mistaken, or forgotten, the Constitution is written. To what purpose are powers limited, and to what purpose is that limitation committed to writing, if these limits may, at any time, be passed by those intended to be restrained? The distinction between a government with limited and unlimited powers is abolished, if those limits do not confine the persons on whom they are imposed, and if acts prohibited and acts allowed are of equal obligation. It is a proposition too plain to be contested, that the Constitution controls any legislative act repugnant to it; or that the legislature may alter the Constitution by an ordinary act.

Between these alternatives there is no middle ground. The Constitution is either a superior paramount law, unchangeable by ordinary means, or it is on a level with ordinary legislative acts, and, like other acts, is alterable when the legislature shall please to alter it.

If the former part of the alternative be true, then a legislative act contrary to the Constitution is not law; if the latter part be true, then written constitutions are absurd attempts, on the part of the people, to limit a power in its own nature illimitable.

Certainly all those who have framed written constitutions contemplate them as forming the fundamental and paramount law of the nation, and, consequently, the theory of every such government must be, that an act of the legislature, repugnant to the Constitution, is void.

This theory is essentially attached to a written constitution, and is consequently to be considered, by this court, as one of the fundamental principles of our society. It is not, therefore, to be lost sight of in the further consideration of this subject.

If an act of the legislature, repugnant to the Constitution is void, does it, notwithstanding its invalidity, bind the courts, and oblige them to give it effect? Or, in other words, though it be not law, does it constitute a rule as operative as if it was a law? This would be to overthrow in fact what was established in theory; and would seem, at first view, an absurdity too gross to be insisted on. It shall, however, receive a more attentive consideration.

It is emphatically the province and duty of the judicial department to say what the law is. Those who apply the rule to particular cases must of necessity expound and interpret that rule. If two laws conflict with each other, the courts must decide on the operation of each.

So if a law be in opposition to the Constitution; if both the law and the Constitution apply to a particular case, so that the court must either decide that case conformably to the law, disregarding the Constitution, or conformably to the Constitution, disregarding the law, the court must determine which of these conflicting rules governs the case. This is of the very essence of judicial duty.

If, then, the courts are to regard the Constitution, and the Constitution is superior to any ordinary act of the legislature, the Constitution, and not such ordinary act, must govern the case to which they both apply.

Those, then, who controvert the principle that the Constitution is to be considered, in court, as a paramount law, are reduced to the necessity of maintaining that courts must close their eyes on the Constitution, and see only the law.

This doctrine would subvert the very foundation of all written constitutions. It would declare that an act which, according to the principles and theory of our government, is entirely void, is yet, in practice, completely obligatory. It would declare that if the legislature shall do what is expressly forbidden, such act, notwithstanding the express prohibition, is in reality effectual. It would be giving to the legislature a practical and real omnipotence, with the same breath which professes to restrict their powers within narrow limits. It is prescribing limits, and declaring that those limits may be passed at pleasure.

That it thus reduces to nothing what we have deemed the greatest improvement on political institutions, a written constitution, would of itself be sufficient, in America, where written constitutions have been viewed with so much reverence, for rejecting the construction. But the peculiar expressions of the Constitution of the United States furnish additional arguments in favor of its rejection.

The judicial power of the United States is extended to all cases arising under the Constitution.

Could it be the intention of those who gave this power, to say that in using it the Constitution should not be looked into? That a case arising under the Constitution should be decided without examining the instrument under which it arises?

This is too extravagant to be maintained.

In some cases, then, the Constitution must be looked into by the judges. And if they can open it at all, what part of it are they forbidden to read or to obey?

There are many other parts of the Constitution which serve to illustrate this subject.

It is declared that "no tax or duty shall be laid on articles exported from any State." Suppose a duty on the export of cotton, of tobacco, or of flour; and a suit instituted to recover it. Ought judgment to be rendered in such a case? ought the judges to close their eyes on the Constitution, and only see the law?

The Constitution declares "that no bill of attainder or *ex post facto* law shall be passed."

If, however, such a bill should be passed, and a person should be prosecuted under it, must the court condemn to death those victims whom the Constitution endeavors to preserve?

"No person," says the Constitution, "shall be convicted of treason unless on the testimony of two witnesses to the same overt act, or on confession in open court."

115

Here the language of the Constitution is addressed especially to the courts. It prescribes, directly for them a rule of evidence not to be departed from. If the legislature should change that rule, and declare one witness, or a confession out of court, sufficient for conviction, must the constitutional principle yield to the legislative act?

From these, and many other selections which might be made, it is apparent that the framers of the Constitution contemplated that instrument as a rule for the government of courts, as well as of the legislature.

Why otherwise does it direct the judges to take an oath to support it? This oath certainly applies in an especial manner to their conduct in their official character. How immoral to impose it on them, if they were to be used as the instruments, and the knowing instruments, for violating what they swear to support!

The oath of office, too, imposed by the legislature, is completely demonstrative of the legislative opinion on this subject. It is in these words: "I do solemnly swear that I will administer justice without respect to persons, and do equal right to the poor and to the rich; and that I will faithfully and impartially discharge all the duties incumbent on me as   , according to the best of my abilities and understanding, agreeably to the Constitution and laws of the United States."

Why does a judge swear to discharge his duties agreeably to the Constitution of the United States, if that Constitution forms no rule for his government—if it is closed upon him, and cannot be inspected by him?

If such be the real state of things, this is worse than solemn mockery. To prescribe, or to take this oath, becomes equally a crime.

It is also not entirely unworthy of observation, that in declaring what shall be the supreme law of the land, the Constitution itself is first mentioned; and not the laws of the United States generally, but those only which shall be made in pursuance of the Constitution, have that rank.

Thus, the particular phraseology of the Constitution of the United States confirms and strengthens the principle, supposed to be essential to all written constitutions, that a law repugnant to the Constitution is void; and that courts, as well as other departments, are bound by that instrument.

116

In the face of the evidence above adduced, in the face of the political doctrines enunciated time and again on divers occasions by the leaders in the Convention, it certainly is incumbent upon those who say that judicial control was not within the purpose of the men who framed and enacted the federal Constitution to bring forward positive evidence, not arguments resting upon silence. It is incumbent upon them to show that the American federal system was not designed primarily to commit the established rights of property to the guardianship of a judiciary removed from direct contact with popular electorates. Whether this system is outworn, whether it has unduly exalted property rights, is a legitimate matter for debate; but those who hold the affirmative cannot rest their case on the intent of the eighteenth-century statesmen who framed the Constitution.

Note on the Views of Thomas Jefferson

The great authority of Jefferson is often used by the opponents of judicial control; and it is true that, after his party was in command of the legislative and executive branches of the government, he frequently attacked judicial "usurpation" with great vehemence. The Federalists were in possession of the Supreme Court for some time after his inauguration. Jefferson was not a member of the convention that drafted the Constitution nor of the Virginia convention that ratified it. There is, however, absolutely no question that at the time the Constitution was formed he favored some kind of direct judicial control. In a letter to Madison, dated Paris, December 20, 1787, he said: "I like the organization of the government into Legislative, Judiciary and Executive . . . And I like the negative given to the Executive with a third of either house, though I should have liked it better had the judiciary been associated for that purpose, or invested with a similar and separate power."[1] He

---

[1] *Writings* (Ford ed.), vol. iv, pp. 475, 476.

had before him, of course, only a copy of the new instrument and
the explanatory letters from his friends. In another letter from
Paris, to F. Hopkinson, he approved the idea of a council of revision
and added "What I disapproved from the first moment also was
the want of a bill of rights to guard liberty against the legislative
as well as executive branches of the government ["by" stricken out
in the manuscript—it would be interesting to know whether he had
in mind "the judiciary"], that is to say, to secure freedom in religion, freedom of the press, freedom from monopolies, *etc.*" [1] Jefferson favored a bill of rights because of "the legal check which it
puts into the hands of the judiciary." [2]

---

[1] *Ibid.*, vol. v, p. 76.
[2] *Ibid.*, vol. v, p. 81.

Appendix

The Constitution

of

The United States

of America

We the People of the United States, in Order to form a more perfect Union, establish Justice, insure domestic Tranquility, provide for the common defence, promote the general Welfare, and secure the Blessings of Liberty to ourselves and our Posterity, do ordain and establish this Constitution for the United States of America.

Article I

Section 1. All legislative Powers herein granted shall be vested in a Congress of the United States, which shall consist of a Senate and House of Representatives.

Section 2. The House of Representatives shall be composed of Members chosen every second Year by the People of the several States, and the Electors in each State shall have the Qualifications requisite for Electors of the most numerous Branch of the State Legislature.

No Person shall be a Representative who shall not have attained to the Age of twenty five Years, and been seven Years a Citizen of the United States, and who shall not, when elected, be an Inhabitant of that State in which he shall be chosen.

Representatives and direct Taxes shall be apportioned among the several States which may be included within this Union, according to their respective Numbers, which shall be determined by adding to the whole Number of free Persons, including those bound to Service for a Term of Years, and excluding Indians not taxed, three fifths of all other Persons. The actual Enumeration shall be made within three Years after the first Meeting of the Congress of the United States, and within every subsequent Term of ten Years, in such Manner as they shall by Law direct. The Number of Representatives shall not exceed one for every thirty Thousand, but each State shall have at Least one Representative; and until such enumeration shall be made, the State of New

121

Hampshire shall be entitled to chuse three, Massachusetts eight, Rhode-Island and Providence Plantations one, Connecticut five, New-York six, New Jersey four, Pennsylvania eight, Delaware one, Maryland six, Virginia ten, North Carolina five, South Carolina five, and Georgia three.

When vacancies happen in the Representation from any State, the Executive Authority thereof shall issue Writs of Election to fill such Vacancies.

The House of Representatives shall chuse their Speaker and other Officers; and shall have the sole Power of Impeachment.

Section 3. The Senate of the United States shall be composed of two Senators from each State, chosen by the Legislature thereof, for six Years; and each Senator shall have one Vote.

Immediately after they shall be assembled in Consequence of the first Election, they shall be divided as equally as may be into three Classes. The Seats of the Senators of the first Class shall be vacated at the Expiration of the second Year, of the second Class at the Expiration of the Fourth Year, and of the third Class at the Expiration of the sixth Year, so that one third may be chosen every second Year; and if Vacancies happen by Resignation, or otherwise, during the Recess of the Legislature of any State, the Executive thereof may make temporary Appointments until the next Meeting of the Legislature, which shall then fill such Vacancies.

No Person shall be a Senator who shall not have attained to the Age of thirty Years, and been nine Years a Citizen of the United States, and who shall not, when elected, be an Inhabitant of that State for which he shall be chosen.

The Vice President of the United States shall be President of the Senate, but shall have no Vote, unless they be equally divided.

The Senate shall chuse their other Officers, and also a President pro tempore, in the Absence of the Vice President, or when he shall exercise the Office of President of the United States.

The Senate shall have the sole Power to try all Impeachments. When sitting for that Purpose, they shall be on Oath or Affirmation. When the President of the United States is tried, the Chief Justice shall preside: And no Person shall be convicted without the Concurrence of two thirds of the Members present.

Judgment in Cases of Impeachment shall not extend further than to removal from Office, and disqualification to hold and enjoy any Office of honor, Trust or Profit under the United States: but the Party convicted shall nevertheless be liable and subject to Indictment, Trial, Judgment and Punishment, according to Law.

Section 4. The Times, Places and Manner of holding Elections for Senators and Representatives, shall be prescribed in each State by the Legislature thereof; but the Congress may at any time by Law make or alter such Regulations, except as to the Places of chusing Senators.

The Congress shall assemble at least once in every Year, and such Meeting shall be on the first Monday in December, unless they shall by Law appoint a different Day.

Section 5. Each House shall be the Judge of the Elections, Returns and Qualifications of its own Members, and a Majority of each shall constitute a Quorum to do Business; but a smaller Number may adjourn from day to day,

122

and may be authorized to compel the Attendance of absent Members, in such Manner, and under such Penalties as each House may provide.

Each House may determine the Rules of its Proceedings, punish its Members for disorderly Behaviour, and, with the Concurrence of two thirds, expel a Member.

Each House shall keep a Journal of its Proceedings, and from time to time publish the same, excepting such Parts as may in their Judgment require Secrecy; and the Yeas and Nays of the Members of either House on any question shall, at the Desire of one fifth of those Present, be entered on the Journal.

Neither House, during the Session of Congress, shall, without the Consent of the other, adjourn for more than three days, nor to any other Place than that in which the two Houses shall be sitting.

Section 6. The Senators and Representatives shall receive a Compensation for their Services, to be ascertained by Law, and paid out of the Treasury of the United States. They shall in all Cases, except Treason, Felony and Breach of the Peace, be privileged from Arrest during their Attendance at the Session of their respective Houses, and in going to and returning from the same; and for any Speech or Debate in either House, they shall not be questioned in any other Place.

No Senator or Representative shall, during the Time for which he was elected, be appointed to any civil Office under the Authority of the United States, which shall have been created, or the Emoluments whereof shall have been encreased during such time; and no Person holding any Office under the United States, shall be a Member of either House during his Continuance in Office.

Section 7. All Bills for raising Revenue shall originate in the House of Representatives; but the Senate may propose or concur with Amendments as on other Bills.

Every Bill which shall have passed the House of Representatives and the Senate, shall, before it become a Law, be presented to the President of the United States; If he approve he shall sign it, but if not he shall return it, with his Objections to that House in which it shall have originated, who shall enter the Objections at large on their Journal, and proceed to reconsider it. If after such Reconsideration two thirds of that House shall agree to pass the Bill, it shall be sent, together with the Objections, to the other House, by which it shall likewise be reconsidered, and if approved by two thirds of that House, it shall become a Law. But in all such Cases the Votes of both Houses shall be determined by yeas and Nays, and the Names of the Persons voting for and against the Bill shall be entered on the Journal of each House respectively. If any Bill shall not be returned by the President within ten Days (Sundays excepted) after it shall have been presented to him, the Same shall be a Law, in like Manner as if he had signed it, unless the Congress by their Adjournment prevent its Return, in which Case it shall not be a Law.

Every Order, Resolution, or Vote to which the Concurrence of the Senate and House of Representatives may be necessary (except on a question of Adjournment) shall be presented to the President of the United States; and before the Same shall take Effect, shall be approved by him, or being disapproved by him, shall be repassed by two thirds of the Senate and House of

Representatives, according to the Rules and Limitations prescribed in the Case of a Bill.

Section 8. The Congress shall have Power To lay and collect Taxes, Duties, Imposts and Excises, to pay the Debts and provide for the common Defence and general Welfare of the United States; but all Duties, Imposts and Excises shall be uniform throughout the United States;

To borrow Money on the credit of the United States;

To regulate Commerce with foreign Nations, and among the several States, and with the Indian Tribes;

To establish an uniform Rule of Naturalization, and uniform Laws on the subject of Bankruptcies throughout the United States;

To coin Money, regulate the Value thereof, and of foreign Coin, and fix the Standard of Weights and Measures;

To provide for the Punishment of counterfeiting the Securities and current Coin of the United States;

To establish Post Offices and post Roads;

To promote the Progress of Science and useful Arts, by securing for limited Times to Authors and Inventors the exclusive Right to their respective Writings and Discoveries;

To constitute Tribunals inferior to the supreme Court;

To define and punish Piracies and Felonies committed on the high Seas, and Offences against the Law of Nations;

To declare War, grant Letters of Marque and Reprisal, and make Rules concerning Captures on Land and Water;

To raise and support Armies, but no Appropriation of Money to that Use shall be for a longer Term than two Years;

To provide and maintain a Navy;

To make Rules for the Government and Regulation of the land and naval Forces;

To provide for calling forth the Militia to execute the Laws of the Union, suppress Insurrections and repel Invasions;

To provide for organizing, arming, and disciplining, the Militia, and for governing such Part of them as may be employed in the Service of the United States, reserving to the States respectively, the Appointment of the Officers, and the Authority of training the Militia according to the discipline prescribed by Congress;

To exercise exclusive Legislation in all Cases whatsoever, over such District (not exceeding ten Miles square) as may, by Cession of particular States, and the Acceptance of Congress, become the Seat of the Government of the United States, and to exercise like Authority over all Places purchased by the Consent of the Legislature of the State in which the Same shall be, for the Erection of Forts, Magazines, Arsenals, dock-Yards, and other needful Buildings;—And

To make all Laws which shall be necessary and proper for carrying into Execution the foregoing Powers, and all other Powers vested by this Constitution in the Government of the United States, or in any Department or Officer thereof.

Section 9. The Migration or Importation of such Persons as any of the States now existing shall think proper to admit, shall not be prohibited by the Congress prior to the Year one thousand eight hundred and eight, but a Tax or duty may be imposed on such Importation, not exceeding ten dollars for each Person.

The Privilege of the Writ of Habeas Corpus shall not be suspended, unless when in Cases of Rebellion or Invasion the public Safety may require it.

No Bill of Attainder or ex post facto Law shall be passed.

No Capitation, or other direct, Tax shall be laid, unless in Proportion to the Census or Enumeration herein before directed to be taken.

No Tax or Duty shall be laid on Articles exported from any State.

No Preference shall be given by any Regulation of Commerce or Revenue to the Ports of one State over those of another: nor shall Vessels bound to, or from, one State, be obliged to enter, clear, or pay Duties in another.

No Money shall be drawn from the Treasury, but in Consequence of Appropriations made by Law; and a regular Statement and Account of the Receipts and Expenditures of all public Money shall be published from time to time.

No Title of Nobility shall be granted by the United States: And no Person holding any Office of Profit or Trust under them, shall, without the Consent of the Congress, accept of any present, Emolument, Office, or Title, of any kind whatever, from any King, Prince, or foreign State.

Section 10. No State shall enter into any Treaty, Alliance, or Confederation; grant Letters of Marque and Reprisal; coin Money; emit Bills of Credit; make any Thing but gold and silver Coin a Tender in Payment of Debts; pass any Bill of Attainder, ex post facto Law, or Law impairing the Obligation of Contracts, or grant any Title of Nobility.

No State shall, without the Consent of the Congress, lay any Imposts or Duties on Imports or Exports, except what may be absolutely necessary for executing it's inspection Laws: and the net Produce of all Duties and Imposts, laid by any State on Imports or Exports, shall be for the Use of the Treasury of the United States; and all such Laws shall be subject to the Revision and Controul of the Congress.

No State shall, without the Consent of Congress, lay any Duty of Tonnage, keep Troops, or Ships of War in time of Peace, enter into any Agreement or Compact with another State, or with a foreign Power, or engage in War, unless actually invaded, or in such imminent Danger as will not admit of delay.

Article II

Section 1. The executive Power shall be vested in a President of the United States of America. He shall hold his Office during the Term of four Years, and, together with the Vice President, chosen for the same Term, be elected, as follows

Each State shall appoint, in such Manner as the Legislature thereof may direct, a Number of Electors, equal to the whole Number of Senators and Representatives to which the State may be entitled in the Congress: but no Senator or Representative, or Person holding an Office of Trust or Profit under the United States, shall be appointed an Elector.

The Electors shall meet in their respective States, and vote by Ballot for two Persons, of whom one at least shall not be an Inhabitant of the same State with themselves. And they shall make a List of all the Persons voted for, and of the Number of Votes for each; which List they shall sign and certify, and transmit sealed to the Seat of the Government of the United States, directed to the President of the Senate. The President of the Senate shall, in the Presence of the Senate and House of Representatives, open all the Certificates, and the Votes shall then be counted. The Person having the greatest Number of Votes shall be the President, if such Number be a Majority of the whole Number of Electors appointed; and if there be more than one who have such Majority, and have an equal Number of Votes, then the House of Representatives shall immediately chuse by Ballot one of them for President; and if no Person have a Majority, then from the five highest on the List the said House shall in like Manner chuse the President. But in chusing the President, the Votes shall be taken by States, the Representation from each State having one Vote; A quorum for this Purpose shall consist of a Member or Members from two thirds of the States, and a Majority of all the States shall be necessary to a Choice. In every Case, after the Choice of the President, the Person having the greatest Number of Votes of the Electors shall be the Vice President. But if there should remain two or more who have equal Votes, the Senate shall chuse from them by Ballot the Vice President.

The Congress may determine the Time of chusing the Electors, and the Day on which they shall give their Votes; which Day shall be the same throughout the United States.

No Person except a natural born Citizen, or a Citizen of the United States, at the time of the Adoption of this Constitution, shall be eligible to the Office of President; neither shall any Person be eligible to that Office who shall not have attained to the Age of thirty five Years, and been fourteen Years a Resident within the United States.

In Case of the Removal of the President from Office, or of his Death, Resignation, or Inability to discharge the Powers and Duties of the said Office, the Same shall devolve on the Vice President, and the Congress may by Law provide for the Case of Removal, Death, Resignation or Inability, both of the President and Vice President, declaring what Officer shall then act as President, and such Officer shall act accordingly, until the Disability be removed, or a President shall be elected.

The President shall, at stated Times, receive for his Services, a Compensation, which shall neither be encreased nor diminished during the Period for which he shall have been elected, and he shall not receive within that Period any other Emolument from the United States, or any of them.

Before he enter on the Execution of his Office, he shall take the following Oath or Affirmation:—"I do solemnly swear (or affirm) that I will faithfully execute the Office of President of the United States, and will to the best of my Ability, preserve, protect and defend the Constitution of the United States."

Section 2. The President shall be Commander in Chief of the Army and Navy of the United States, and of the Militia of the several States, when called into the actual Service of the United States; he may require the Opinion, in writing, of the principal Officer in each of the executive Departments, upon any Subject relating to the Duties of their respective Offices, and he shall have Power to grant Reprieves and Pardons for Offences against the United States, except in Cases of Impeachment.

He shall have Power, by and with the Advice and Consent of the Senate, to make Treaties, providing two thirds of the Senators present concur; and he shall nominate, and by and with the Advice and Consent of the Senate, shall appoint Ambassadors, other public Ministers and Consuls, Judges of the supreme Court, and all other Officers of the United States, whose Appointments are not herein otherwise provided for, and which shall be established by Law: but the Congress may by Law vest the Appointment of such inferior Officers, as they think proper, in the President alone, in the Courts of Law, or in the Heads of Departments.

The President shall have Power to fill up all Vacancies that may happen during the Recess of the Senate by granting Commissions which shall expire at the End of their next Session.

Section 3. He shall from time to time give to the Congress Information of the State of the Union, and recommend to their Consideration such Measures as he shall judge necessary and expedient; he may, on extraordinary Occasions, convene both Houses, or either of them, and in Case of Disagreement between them, with Respect to the Time of Adjournment, he may adjourn them to such Time as he shall think proper; he shall receive Ambassadors and other public Ministers; he shall take Care that the Laws be faithfully executed, and shall Commission all the Officers of the United States.

Section 4. The President, the Vice President and all civil Officers of the United States, shall be removed from Office on Impeachment for, and Conviction of, Treason, Bribery, or other high Crimes and Misdemeanors.

Article III

Section 1. The judicial Power of the United States, shall be vested in one supreme Court, and in such inferior Courts as the Congress may from time to time ordain and establish. The Judges, both of the supreme and inferior Courts, shall hold their Offices during good Behaviour, and shall, at stated Times, receive for their Services, a Compensation, which shall not be diminished during their Continuance in Office.

Section 2. The judicial Power shall extend to all Cases, in Law and Equity, arising under this Constitution, the Laws of the United States, and Treaties made, or which shall be made, under their Authority;—to all Cases affecting Ambassadors, other public Ministers and Consuls;—to all Cases of admiralty and maritime Jurisdiction;—to Controversies to which the United States shall be a Party;—to Controversies between two or more States;—between a State and Citizens of another State;—between Citizens of different States;—between Citizens of the same State claiming Lands under Grants of different States, and between a State, or the Citizens thereof, and foreign States, Citizens or Subjects.

In all Cases affecting Ambassadors, other public Ministers and Consuls, and those in which a State shall be Party, the supreme Court shall have original Jurisdiction. In all the other Cases before mentioned, the supreme Court shall have appellate Jurisdiction, both as to Law and Fact, with such Exceptions, and under such Regulations as the Congress shall make.

The Trial of all Crimes, except in Cases of Impeachment, shall be by Jury; and such Trial shall be held in the State where the said Crimes shall have been committed; but when not committed within any State, the Trial shall be at such Place or Places as the Congress may by Law have directed.

Section 3. Treason against the United States, shall consist only in levying War against them, or adhering to their Enemies, giving them Aid and Comfort. No Person shall be convicted of Treason unless on the Testimony of two Witnesses to the same overt Act, or on Confession in open Court.

The Congress shall have Power to declare the Punishment of Treason, but no Attainder of Treason shall work Corruption of Blood, or Forfeiture except during the Life of the Person attainted.

Article IV

Section 1. Full Faith and Credit shall be given in each State to the public Acts, Records, and judicial Proceedings of every other State. And the Congress may by general Laws prescribe the Manner in which such Acts, Records and Proceedings shall be proved, and the Effect thereof.

Section 2. The Citizens of each State shall be entitled to all Privileges and Immunities of Citizens in the several States.

A Person charged in any State with Treason, Felony, or other Crime, who shall flee from Justice, and be found in another State, shall on Demand of the executive Authority of the State from which he fled, be delivered up, to be removed to the State having Jurisdiction of the Crime.

No Person held to Service or Labour in one State, under the Laws thereof, escaping into another, shall, in Consequence of any Law or Regulation therein, be discharged from such Service or Labour, but shall be delivered up on Claim of the Party to whom such Service or Labour may be due.

Section 3. New States may be admitted by the Congress into this Union; but no new State shall be formed or erected within the Jurisdiction of any other State; nor any State be formed by the Junction of two or more States, or Parts of States, without the Consent of the Legislatures of the States concerned as well as of the Congress.

The Congress shall have Power to dispose of and make all needful Rules and Regulations respecting the Territory or other Property belonging to the United States; and nothing in this Constitution shall be so construed as to Prejudice any Claims of the United States, or of any particular State.

Section 4. The United States shall guarantee to every State in this Union a Republican Form of Government, and shall protect each of them against Invasion; and on Application of the Legislature, or of the Executive (when the Legislature cannot be convened) against domestic Violence.

Article V

The Congress, whenever two thirds of both Houses shall deem it necessary, shall propose Amendments to this Constitution, or, on the Application of the Legislatures of two thirds of the several States, shall call a Convention for proposing Amendments, which, in either Case, shall be valid to all Intents and Purposes, as Part of this Constitution, when ratified by the Legislatures of three fourths of the several States, or by Conventions in three fourths thereof, as the one or the other Mode of Ratification may be proposed by the Congress; Provided that no Amendment which may be made prior to the Year One thousand eight hundred and eight shall in any Manner affect the first and fourth Clauses in the Ninth Section of the first Article; and that no State, without its Consent, shall be deprived of its equal Suffrage in the Senate.

Article VI

All Debts contracted and Engagements entered into, before the Adoption of this Constitution, shall be as valid against the United States under this Constitution, as under the Confederation.

This Constitution, and the Laws of the United States which shall be made in Pursuance thereof; and all Treaties made, or which shall be made, under the Authority of the United States, shall be the supreme Law of the Land; and the Judges in every State shall be bound thereby, any Thing in the Constitution or Laws of any State to the Contrary notwithstanding.

The Senators and Representatives before mentioned, and the Members of the several State Legislatures, and all executive and judicial Officers, both of the United States and of the several States, shall be bound by Oath or Affirmation, to support this Constitution; but no religious Test shall ever be required as a Qualification to any Office or public Trust under the United States.

Article VII

The Ratification of the Conventions of nine States, shall be sufficient for the Establishment of this Constitution between the States so ratifying the Same.

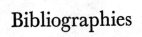

Bibliographies

An Historical Bibliography
on the Supreme Court's Authority
to Pass upon the Constitutionality
of Congressional Acts

This bibliography does not list all or even most of the books and articles dealing with the exercise of judicial review by the Supreme Court. The focus here is on legal and public debate over the Court's power to review Congressional acts, in each of the major periods and sub-periods discussed in the essay, "Charles Beard and American Debate Over Judicial Review, 1790-1961." For each of these periods, works have been selected which indicate the range, intensity, and depth of debate over the Court's possession and use of this power.

I. The Age of "Political Debate," 1790-1880

Butler, George B., "Congress and the Supreme Court," 36 *Harper's New Mon. M.* 657 (1868).

Curtis, Benjamin R. *Jurisdiction, Practice, and Peculiar Jurisprudence of the Courts of the United States.* Boston: Little Brown & Co., 1880.

Curtis, George T. *Commentaries on the Jurisdiction, Practice, and Peculiar Jurisprudence of the Courts of the United States.* Philadelphia: T. & W. Johnson, 1854.

Duponceau, Peter S. *A Dissertation on the Nature and Extent of the Jurisdiction of the Courts of the United States.* Philadelphia: Abraham Small, 1824.

Dutton, Warren, "Constitutional Law," 10 *N. Am. Rev.* 115 (1820).

Elliot, Jonathan. *The Debates in the Several State Conventions on the Adoption of the Federal Constitution.* Washington: The Editor, 1827-30.

Kent, James. *Commentaries on American Law.* New York: O. Halsted, 1826.

Madison, James. *Journal of the Federal Convention.* Washington: Langtree & O'Sullivan, 1840.

Pomeroy, John N. *An Introduction to the Constitutional Law of the United States,* 3rd ed. New York: Hurd & Houghton, 1877.

Rawle, William. *A View of the Constitution of the United States of America,* 2nd ed. Philadelphia: Philip Nicklin, 1829.

Story, Joseph. *Commentaries on the Constitution of the United States.* Boston: Hilliard Gray, 1833.

Tiffany, Joel. *A Treatise on Government and Constitutional Law.* Albany, N.Y.: W. C. Little, 1867.

Towle, Nathaniel. *A History and Analysis of the Constitution of the United States,* 3rd ed. Boston: Little, Brown & Co., 1871.

Wilson, James. *The Works of the Hon. James Wilson.* Philadelphia: Bronson & Chauncey, 1804.

Anon., "The Tribunal of Dernier Resort," 6 *So. L. Rev.* 421 (1830).

Anon., "The Supreme Court of the United States," 2 *N.Y. Rev.* 372 (1838).

Anon., "The Supreme Court of the United States," 24 *Liv. Age* 550 (1850).

(Note: Most of the literature in addition to the above items for the pre-Civil War period appears in the newspapers. For generous references to these debates, see Charles Warren, *The Supreme Court in United States History.* Boston: Little, Brown, & Co., 1922.

II. *The Age of Historical Debate, 1880-1920*

Traditionalist Debate on Historical Lines, 1880-1900

Akin, John W., "Aggressions of the Federal Courts," 32 *Am. L. Rev.* 669 (1898).

Allen, Lafon, "An Answer to Gov. Pennoyer," 29 *Am. L. Rev.* 847 (1895).

Anderson, F. M., "Contemporary Opinion of the Virginia and Kentucky Resolutions," 5 *Am. Hist. Rev.* 45 (1899).

Bancroft, George. *History of the Formation of the Constitution of the United States of America.* New York: D. Appleton & Co., 1882.

———. *A Plea for the Constitution of the United States of America, Wounded in the House of its Guardians.* New York, 1886.

Bonney, G. C., "Judicial Supremacy," 16 *Chi. L. News* 6 (1884).

Brown, T. W., "Due Process of Law," 32 *Am. L. Rev.* 14 (1898).

Burke, N. C., "The Charge of Judicial Usurpation," 60 *Ohio L. Bull.* 385 (1916).

Butler, William A., "The Origin of the Supreme Court of the United States and its Place in the Constitution," in *The Supreme Court of the United States,* ed. Hampton L. Carson. Philadelphia: John Y. Yuber, 1891.

Carson, Hampton L., "Judicial Power and Unconstitutional Legislation," 34 *Am. L. Rev.* 796 (1900).

Coles, Walter D., "Politics and the Supreme Court of the United States," 27 *Am. L. Rev.* 183 (1893).

Cooley, Thomas M. *Constitutional History of the United States.* New York: G. P. Putnam's Sons, 1889.

Coxe, Brinton. *An Essay on Judicial Power and Unconstitutional Legislation.* Philadelphia: Kay & Brother, 1893.

Davis, Andrew M., "The Case of Frost v. Leighton," 2 *Am. Hist. Rev.* 229 (1897).

Doolittle, James R., "The Veto Power of the Supreme Court," 1 *Chi. L. Times* 177 (1887).

HISTORICAL BIBLIOGRAPHY

Elliott, Charles B., "The Legislatures and the Courts: The Power to Declare Statutes Unconstitutional," 5 *Pol. Sci. Q.* 224 (1890).

Farrand, Max, "The Judiciary Act of 1801," 5 *Am. Hist. Rev.* 682 (1900).

Flanders, Henry, "Has the Supreme Court of the United States the Constitutional Power to Declare Void an Act of Congress?" 48 *Am. L. Reg.* 35 (1900).

Fowler, Robert L., "The Origin of the Supreme Judicial Power in the Federal Constitution," 29 *Am. L. Rev.* 711 (1895).

Hazeltine, H. D., "Appeals from Colonial Courts to the King in Council," in *Report of the American Historical Association* (1894), 299.

Hearst, William R., "The Supreme Court Versus the People," 1 *Law Mag.* 35 (1913).

Herbert, Hilary A., "The Supreme Court of the United States and its Functions," *Report of the Pennsylvania Bar Association,* 3rd Annual Meeting, 1897, 155.

Jameson, John F. *Essays on the Constitutional History of the United States in the Formative Period,* 1775-1789. Boston: Houghton Mifflin Company, 1889.

McMurtrie, Richard C. *Plea for the Supreme Court: Observations on Mr. George Bancroft's Plea for the Constitution.* Philadelphia, 1886.

————., "The Jurisdiction to Declare Void Acts of Legislation," 32 *Am. Law Reg.* n.s. 1093 (1893).

Meigs, William M., "The Relation of the Judiciary to the Constitution," 19 *Am. L. Rev.* 174 (1885).

Parker, Junius, "The Supreme Court and its Constitutional Duty and Power," 30 *Am. L. Rev.* 357 (1896).

Pennoyer, Sylvester, "The Income Tax Decision and the Power of the Supreme Court to Nullify Acts of Congress," 29 *Am. L. Rev.* 550 (1895).

————., "A Reply," 29 *Am. L. Rev.* 857 (1895).

————., "The Power of the Supreme Court to Declare an Act of Congress Unconstitutional: The Case of Marbury v. Madison," 30 *Am. L. Rev.* 183 (1896).

Phelps, Edward J., "The Supreme Court and the Sovereignty of the People," in *The Supreme Court of the United States,* ed. Hampton L. Carson. Philadelphia: John Y. Yuber, 1891, p. 690.

Rosenberger, T. C., "The Supreme Court as Expounder of the Constitution," 30 *Am. L. Rev.* 55 (1896).

Scott, Austin, "Holmes v. Walton: the New Jersey Precedent," 4 *Am. Hist. Rev.* 456 (1899).

Street, Robert G., "How Far Questions of Policy May Enter into Judicial Decisions," 6 A.B.A.J 179 (1883).

Thayer, James B., "The Origin and Scope of the American Doctrine of Constitutional Law," 7 *Harv. L. Rev.* 129 (1893).

Tiedeman, Christopher G. *The Unwritten Constitution of the United States.* New York: Putnam, 1890.

Wilson, John R., "The Origin of the Power of Courts to Declare Legislative Acts Unconstitutional," *Report of the Indiana State Bar Association* (1899), 12.

Winchester, Boyd, "The Judiciary: Its Growing Power and Influence," 32 *Am. L. Rev.* 801 (1898).

The New Critics and the New Defenders, 1901-1920

Adams, Brooks. *The Theory of Social Revolutions*. New York: The Macmillan Co., 1913.

Alger, George W. *The Old Law and the New Social Order*. Boston: Houghton Mifflin Company, 1913.

Baldwin, Simeon. *The American Judiciary*. New York: The Century Co., 1905.

Ballantine, Henry W., "Labor Legislation and the Recall of the Judicial Veto," 19 *Case and Comment* 225 (1912).

Beard, Charles A., "The Supreme Court: Usurper or Grantee?", 27 *Pol. Sci. Q.* 1 (1912).

———. *The Supreme Court and the Constitution*. New York: The Macmillan Co., 1912.

Beck, James M.. "Nullification by Indirection," 23 *Harv. L. Rev.* 441 (1910).

Benson, Allan L., "The Usurped Power of the Courts," 16 *Pearson's Mag.* (1911).

Biggs, J. Crawford, "The Power of the Judiciary Over Legislation," 13 *Proceedings of the N. Car. Bar Assoc.* (1915).

Bizzell, William B. *Judicial Interpretation of Political Theory*. New York: G. P. Putnam, 1914.

Bordwell, Percy, "The Function of the Judiciary," 7 *Col. L. Rev.* 308, 520 (1907).

Boudin, Louis B., "Government by Judiciary," 26 *Pol. Sci. Q.* 238 (1911).

Bowman, Harold, "Congress and the Supreme Court," 25 *Pol. Sci. Q.* 20 (1910).

Burr, Charles H., "Unconstitutional Laws and the Federal Judicial Power," 60 *U. of Pa. L. Rev.* 624 (1912).

Carson, Hampton L., "The Historic Relation of Judicial Power to Unconstitutional Legislation," 60 *U. of Pa. L. Rev.* 687 (1912).

Carter, Orrin N., "The Courts and Unconstitutional Law," *Proceedings of the Illinois State Bar Assoc.* (1912), 401.

Choate, Joseph H., "The Supreme Court of the United States: Its Place in the Constitution," 176 *N. Am. Rev.* 927 (1903).

Clark, Inglis A., "The Supremacy of the Constitution," 17 *Harv. L. Rev.* 1 (1903).

Clark, Walter, "Is the Supreme Court Constitutional?" 63 *Indep.* 723 (1907).

———, "Government by Judges," 11 *Ohio L. Reporter* 485 (1914).

———, "Where Does the Governing Power Reside?" 52 *Am. L. Rev.* 687 (1918).

———, "Back to the Constitution," 50 *Am. L. Rev.* 1 (1916).

Cohen, Morris R., "The Process of Judicial Legislation," 48 *Am. L. Rev.* 161 (1914).

Corwin, Edward S., "The Supreme Court and Unconstitutional Acts of Congress," 4 *Mich. L. Rev.* 616 (1906).

———, "The Establishment of Judicial Review," 9 *Mich. L. Rev.* 102, 283 (1910).

———, "The Basic Doctrine of American Constitutional Law," 12 *Mich. L. Rev.* 247 (1914).

——, "Marbury v. Madison and the Doctrine of Judicial Review," 12 *Mich. L. Rev.* 538 (1914).

——. *The Doctrine of Judicial Review.* Princeton, N.J.: Princeton University Press, 1914.

Countryman, Edwin. *The Supreme Court of the United States.* Albany, N.Y.: Matthew Bender, 1913.

Davis, Horace A., "Annulment of Legislation by the Supreme Court," 7 *Am. Pol. Sci. Rev.* 541 (1913).

——. *The Judicial Veto.* Boston: Houghton Mifflin Company, 1914.

Dodd, Walter F., "The Growth of Judicial Power," 24 *Pol. Sci. Q.* 193 (1909).

Dougherty, J. Hamden. *The Power of the Federal Judiciary over Legislation.* New York: G. P. Putnam, 1912.

Esterline, Blackburn, The Supreme Law of the Land," 40 *Am. L. Rev.* 566 (1906).

Farrand, Max, "The First Hayburn Case," 13 *Am. Hist. Rev.* 281 (1908).

Goodnow, Frank J., "Judicial Interpretation of Constitutional Provisions," 3 *Proceedings of the Academy of Political Science* (1913), 49.

——. *Social Reform and the Court.* New York: The Macmillan Co., 1911.

Green, Frederick, "The Judicial Censorship of Legislation," 47 *Am. L. Rev.* 90 (1913).

Groat, George G. *Attitude of American Courts in Labor Cases.* New York: Longmans, Green & Co., Inc., 1911.

Guthrie, William D., "Constitutional Morality," 18 *Reports of the Pennsylvania Bar Assoc.* (1912), 331.

Hadley, Arthur T., "The Constitutional Position of Property," 64 *Indep.* 834 (1908).

Haines, Charles G., "Judicial Criticisms of Legislation by Courts," 11 *Mich. L. Rev.* 26 (1912).

——. *The Conflict Over Judicial Powers in the United States to 1870.* (Columbia University Studies, Vol. XXXV, No. 1.), New York, 1909.

——. *The American Doctrine of Judicial Supremacy.* New York, 1914.

Hallam, Oscar, "Judicial Power to Declare Legislative Acts Void," 48 *Am. L. Rev.* 85, 225 (1914).

Hastings, W. G., "Is It Usurpation to Hold as Void Unconstitutional Laws?" 20 *Green Bag* 100 (1908).

Hazeltine, H. D., "Influence of Magna Carta on American Constitutional Development," 7 *Col. L. Rev.* 1 (1917).

Judson, Frederick N. *The Judiciary and the People.* New Haven, Conn.: Yale University Press, 1913.

Kales, Albert M., "The Recall of Judicial Decisions," *Proceedings of the Illinois State Bar Assoc.* (1912), 203.

Lewis, William D., "A New Method of Constitutional Amendment by Popular Vote," 43 *Annals* 311 (1912).

Long, Joseph R., "Unconstitutional Acts of Congress," 1 *Va. L. Rev.* 417 (1914).

Lurton, Horace H., "A Government of Law or of Men," 193 *N. Am. Rev.* 9 (1911).

Maynard, Fred A., "Five to Four Decisions of the Supreme Court of the United States," 89 *Central L. Jour.* 206 (1919).

McClain, Emlin, "Unwritten Constitutions in the United States," 15 *Harv. L. Rev.* 531 (1902).

McDonough, James B., "The Alleged Usurpation of Power by the Federal Courts," 46 *Am. L. Rev.* 45 (1912).

McLaughlin, Andrew C. *The Courts, the Constitution, and Parties.* Chicago: University of Chicago Press, 1912.

Meigs, William M., "The American Doctrine of Judicial Power in its Early Origin," 47 *Am. L. Rev.* 693 (1913).

———, "Some Recent Attacks on the American Doctrine of Judicial Power," 40 *Am. L. Rev.* 640 (1916).

———. *The Relation of the Judiciary to the Constitution.* New York: Neale, 1919.

Melvin, Frank E., "The Judicial Bulwark of the Constitution," 8 *Am. Pol. Sci. Rev.* 167 (1914).

Moore, Blaine F. *The Supreme Court and Unconstitutional Legislation.* (Columbia University Studies, Vol. LIV, No. 2.), New York, 1913.

———, "The Supreme Court and Unconstitutional Legislation," *Am. Pol. Sci. Rev.* 132 (1914).

———, "Judicial Veto and Political Democracy," 10 *Am. Pol. Sci. Rev.* 700 (1916).

Myers, Gustavus. *History of the Supreme Court of the United States.* Chicago: C. H. Kerr, 1912.

Owen, Robert L., "Withdrawing Power from the Federal Courts to Declare Acts of Congress Void," U.S. Senate, 64th Cong., 2d Sess, Senate Doc. 737 (1917).

Palfrey, John G., "The Constitution and the Courts," 26 *Harv. L. Rev.* 507 (1913).

Pope, Herbert, "The Fundamental Law and the Courts," 27 *Harv. L. Rev.* 45 (1913).

Patterson, Carum, "Judicial Usurpation of Power," 10 *Va. L. Reg.* 885 (1905).

Pound, Roscoe, "Courts and Legislation," 7 *Am. Pol. Sci. Rev.* 361 (1913).

Ransom, William L. *Majority Rule and the Judiciary.* New York: Charles Scribner's Sons, 1912.

Richter, A. W., "Legislative Curb on the Judiciary," 21 *J. of Pol. Econ.* 281 (1913).

Roe, Gilbert E., *Our Judicial Oligarchy.* New York: B. W. Huebsch, 1912.

Sargent, Noel, "American Judicial Veto," 51 *Am. L. Rev.* 663 (1917).

Schlesinger, Arthur M., "Colonial Appeals to the Privy Council," 28 *Pol. Sci. Q.* 279, 433 (1912).

Sherman, Gordon E., "The Case of John Chandler v. the Secretary of War," 14 *Yale L. J.* 431 (1905).

Smalley, Harrison S., "Nullifying the Law by Judicial Interpretation," 107 *Atl. Mon.* 452 (1911).

Smith, James Allen. *The Spirit of American Government.* New York: The Macmillan Co., 1907.

Snow, Alpheus H., "The Position of the Judiciary in the United States," 43 *Annals* 286 (1912).

HISTORICAL BIBLIOGRAPHY

Street, Robert G., "The Irreconcilable Conflict," 41 *Am. L. Rev.* 686 (1907).

Stuart, Charles B., "Power of the Supreme Court to Declare Acts of Congress Unconstitutional," U.S. Senate, 64th Cong., 2d Sess, Senate Doc. 708 (1917).

Sutherland, William A., "Politics and the Supreme Court," 48 *Am. L. Rev.* 390 (1914).

Taft, William H., *Popular Government.* New Haven, Conn.: Yale University Press, 1913.

Trickett, William, "The Great Usurpation," 40 *Am. L. Rev.* 356 (1906).

——, "Judicial Nullification of Acts of Congress," 185 *N. Am. Rev.* 848 (1907).

——, "Judicial Dispensation from Congressional Statutes," 41 *Am. L. Rev.* 65 (1907).

Turner, Jesse, "A Phantom Precedent," 48 *Am. L. Rev.* 321 (1914).

——, "Four Fugitive Cases From American Constitutional Law," 49 *Am. L. Rev.* 818 (1915).

Wanamaker, R. M., "The Recall of Judges," *Proceedings of the Illinois State Bar Assoc.* (1912), 174.

Warren, Charles, "Legislative and Judicial Attacks on the Supreme Court of the United States," 47 *Am. L. Rev.* 1, 161 (1913).

——, "The Progressiveness of the United States Supreme Court," 13 *Col. L. Rev.* 290 (1913).

Watson, David K., "Power of the Federal Judiciary to Declare Legislation Invalid Which Conflicts With the Federal Constitution," 13 *Ohio L. Rep.* 469 (1915).

Williams, George W., "The Power of Courts to Declare a Statute Void," 52 *Am. L. Rev.* 497 (1918).

Woodward, John, "The Courts and the People," 7 *Col. L. Rev.* 559 (1907).

III. The Era of Critical Realism, 1920-1961

Debate in the Decade of "Normalcy," 1920-1930

Barnett, James D., "External Evidence of the Constitutionality of Statutes," 58 *Am. L. Rev.* 88 (1924).

Bent, James A. *The Independent Judiciary.* Morgantown, W. Va.: Morgantown Printing Co., 1925.

Brown, Douglas W., "The Proposal to Give Congress Power to Nullify the Constitution," 57 *Am. L. Rev.* 161 (1923).

Bruce, Andrew A. *The American Judge.* New York: The Macmillan Co., 1924.

Clark, Walter, "Judicial Veto Wholly Without Authority in the Constitution," 28 *Am. Fed.* 723 (1921).

Clarke, John H., "Judicial Power to Declare Legislation Unconstitutional," 9 *A.B.A.J.* 689 (1923).

Corwin, Edward S., "Judicial Review in Action," 74 *U. of Pa. L. Rev.* 639 (1926).

——, "The Progress of Constitutional Theory Between the Declaration of Independence and the Meeting of the Philadelphia Convention," 30 *Am. Hist. Rev.* 511 (1925).

139

————. *John Marshall and the Constitution.* New Haven, Conn.: Yale University Press, 1921.

Cushman, Robert E., "Constitutional Decisions by a Bare Majority of the Court," 19 *Mich. L. Rev.* 771 (1921).

Dodd, Walter F., "The Judicial Function in Construing a Written Constitution," 4 *Ill. L. Q.* 219 (1922).

Eschweiler, F. C., "The Veto Power of the Judiciary," 7 *Marq L. Rev.* 5 (1922).

Ettrude, Dormin J., ed. *The Power of Congress to Nullify Supreme Court Decisions.* New York: H. W. Wilson Co., 1924.

Finkelstein, Maurice, "Judicial Self-Limitation," 37 *Harv. L. Rev.* 338 (1924).

Ford, John, "Judicial Usurpation," 30 *Am. Fed.* 306 (1923).

Gompers, Samuel, "Take Away its Usurped Power," 30 *Am. Fed.* 399 (1923).

Grinnell, F. W., "Some Forgotten History About the Duty of Courts in Dealing With Unconstitutional Legislation," 54 *Am. L. Rev.* 419 (1920).

Haines, Charles G., "Histories of the Supreme Court of the United States Written From the Federalist Point of View," 4 *Southwestern Pol. & Soc. Sci. Q.* 1 (1923).

————, "A Government of Laws of a Government of Men: Judicial or Legislative Supremacy," Faculty Lecture, 1929, University of California, Los Angeles.

Harris, Lawrence T., "Guardians of the Constitution," 2 *Ore. L. Rev.* 73 (1923).

Hill, David J., "The Assault on the Constitution and the Courts," 9 *Const. Rev.* 12 (1925).

Hughes, Charles Evans. *The Supreme Court of the United States.* New York: Columbia University Press, 1928.

Jiggits, Louis M., "The Supreme Court Under Fire," 41 *L. Quar. Rev.* 95 (1925).

London, Meyer, "Veto Power of the Supreme Court," 30 *Am. Fed.* 224 (1923).

McLaughlin, Andrew C., "Marbury v. Madison Again," 14 *A.B.A.J.* 156 (1928).

Miller, David H., "Some Early Cases in the Supreme Court of the United States," 8 *Va. L. Rev.* 108 (1921).

Monroe, Alan H., "The Supreme Court and the Constitution," 18 *Am. Pol. Sci. Rev.* 737 (1924).

Norton, Thomas J., "Supreme Court's Five to Four Decisions," 9 *A.B.A.J.* 417 (1923).

————. *Losing Liberty Judicially.* New York: The Macmillan Co., 1928.

Pillsbury, Warren H., "The Power of the Courts to Declare Laws Unconstitutional," 11 *Cal. L. Rev.* 313 (1923).

Plunknett, Theodore F. J., "Bonham's Case and Judicial Review," 40 *Harv. L. Rev.* 30 (1926).

Potter, William W.. "Judicial Power in the United States," 27 *Mich. L. Rev.* 1, 167, 285 (1928).

Pound, Cuthbert, "The Judicial Power," 35 *Harv. L. Rev.* 787 (1922).

Ralston, Jackson H., "Judicial Control Over Legislatures as to Constitutional Questions," 44 *Am. L. Rev.* 193 (1920).

Roosevelt, Theodore, Editorials, *The Outlook,* Dec. 17, 1910; Apr. 15, 1911; Jan. 6, Feb. 24, Mar. 21, 1912.

Rubin, W. B., "The Constitution and the Supreme Court," 29 *Am. Fed.* 675 (1922).

Russell, Elmer B. *The Review of American Colonial Legislation by the King in Council.* New York, 1915.

Severance, C. A., "Proposal to Make Congress Supreme," 8 *A.B.A.J.* 459 (1922).

Stinson, J. W., "Marshall and the Supremacy of the Unwritten Law," 58 *Am. L. Rev.* 856 (1924).

Stone, Harlan F., "Fifty Years Work of the United States Supreme Court," 14 *A.B.A.J.* 428 (1928).

Von Moschzisker, Robert. *Judicial Review of Legislation.* Washington: National Association for Constitutional Government, 1923.

Warren, Charles, "New Light on the History of the Federal Judiciary Act of 1789," 37 *Harv. L. Rev.* 49 (1923).

———, "The Early History of the Supreme Court of the United States, in Connection with Modern Attacks on the Judiciary," 8 *Mass. L. Q.* 1 (1923).

———. *The Supreme Court in United States History.* Boston: Little, Brown & Co., 1922.

———. *Congress, the Constitution and the Supreme Court.* Boston: Little, Brown & Co., 1925.

Wheeler, Everett P., "Judicial Power to Declare Legislation Unconstitutional," 10 *A.B.A.J.* 29 (1924).

Debate During the Depression Crisis and the New Deal Response, 1930-1941

Alfange, Dean. *The Supreme Court and the National Will.* New York: Doubleday, Doran & Company, Inc., 1937.

Alsop, Joseph. *The 168 Days.* New York: Doubleday, Doran & Company, Inc., 1938.

Angell, Ernest. *Supreme Court Primer.* New York: Reynal & Hitchcock, Inc., 1937.

Barnes, William R., and A. W. Littlefield, eds. *The Supreme Court Issue and the Constitution.* New York: Barnes & Noble, Inc., 1937.

Beard, Charles, "Social Change and the Constitution," 42 *Cur. Hist.* 345 (1935).

———, "What About the Constitution?" 142 *Nation* 405 (1936).

———, "Economic Bias of Judges in Decisions," 19 *New Leader* 5 (1936).

———, "Little Alice Looks at the Constitution," 87 *New Rep.* 315 (1936).

———, "Rendezvous With the Supreme Court," 88 *New Rep.* 92 (1936).

Borah, William E., "Our Supreme Judicial Tribunal," 3 *Vital Speeches* 258 (1937).

Boudin, Louis B., *Government by Judiciary.* New York: William Godwin, Inc., 1932.

——, "The Constitution and the Supreme Court," 5 *Am. Socialist Mon.* 38 (1936).

Brant, Irving. *Storm over the Constitution.* New York: The Bobbs-Merrill Company, Inc., 1937.

Carr, Robert K. *Democracy and the Supreme Court.* Norman, Okla.: University of Oklahoma Press, 1936.

——. *The Supreme Court and Judicial Review.* New York: Farrar & Rinehart, Inc., 1942.

Clark, Charles E., "Supreme—Court or People?" 6 *Am. Scholar* 201 (1937).

Clark, Grenville, "The Supreme Court Issue," 26 *Yale Rev.* n.s. 669 (1937).

Cooper, Charles P. *The Power of the Supreme Court of the United States to Declare Acts of Congress Void.* Jacksonville, Fla.: Cooper Press, 1935.

Corwin, Edward S. *Court over Constitution.* Princeton, N.J.: Princeton University Press, 1938.

——. *The Twilight of the Supreme Court.* New Haven, Conn.: Yale University Press, 1937.

——. *Constitutional Revolution, Ltd.* Claremont, Calif.: Claremont College, 1941.

——, "Curbing the Court," 2 *Vital Speeches* 373 (1936).

Doar, W. T., "Power of the Courts to Declare Laws Unconstitutional," 1933 *Wisconsin State Bar Association Journal,* 15.

Donovan, William J., "An Independent Supreme Court and the Protection of Minority Rights," 23 *A.B.A.J.* 254 (1937).

Duffy, A. A., "An Early Chapter in the History of Judicial Review," 71 *U.S. L. Rev.* 516 (1937).

Edgerton, Henry W., "The Incidence of Judicial Control Over Congress," 22 *Corn. L. Q.* 299 (1937).

Elliott, William Y. *The Need for Constitutional Reform.* New York: Whittlesey House, 1935.

Ernst, Morris. *The Ultimate Power.* Garden City, N.Y.: Doubleday, Doran & Company, Inc., 1937.

Eriksson, Erik M. *The Supreme Court and the New Deal.* Rosemead, Calif.: Rosemead Review Press, 1940.

Fraenkel, Osmund K., "What Can Be Done About the Constitution and the Supreme Court?" 37 *Col. L. Rev.* 212 (1937).

Frease, Harry. *The Judicial Aftermath of a Political Paradox.* Philadelphia: Winston, 1935.

Grove, Edward, "What Shall Socialists Do About the Supreme Court?" 5 *Am. Socialist Mon.* 15 (1937).

Haines, Charles G., *The Revival of Natural Law Concepts.* Cambridge, Mass.: Harvard University Press, 1930.

——, "Judicial Review of Acts of Congress and the Need for Constitutional Reform," 45 *Yale L. J.* 816 (1936).

Hamilton, Walton, and Douglass Adair. *The Power to Govern.* New York: W. W. Norton & Company, Inc., 1937.

Harriman, E. A., "The Supreme Court and the Unwritten Law," 17 *B.U.L. Rev.* 388 (1937).

Hatcher, J. H., "Power of the Federal Courts to Declare Acts of Congress Unconstitutional," 22 *A.B.A.J.* 163 (1936).

Henry, John M. *Nine Men Above the Law.* Pittsburgh: R. T. Lewis, 1936.

Jackson, Robert H. *The Struggle for Judicial Supremacy.* New York: Alfred A. Knopf, Inc., 1941.

Johnsen, Julia E., ed. *Limitation of the Power of the Supreme Court to Declare Acts of Congress Unconstitutional.* New York: H. W. Wilson Co., 1935.

———. *Reorganization of the Supreme Court.* New York: H. W. Wilson Co., 1937.

Kerr, Charles, "The Thirty Years' War on the Supreme Court," 17 *Va. L. Rev.* 629 (1931).

Landis, James, "Power the Court Has Appropriated," 3 *Vital Speeches* 358 (1937).

LaFollette, Robert M., "Backing the President's Court Proposal," 3 *Vital Speeches* 311 (1937).

Lawrence, David. *Nine Honest Men.* New York: D. Appleton Century, 1936.

———. *Supreme Court or Political Puppets.* New York: D. Appleton Century Company, Inc., 1937.

Lerner, Max, "The Supreme Court and American Capitalism," 42 *Yale L. J.* 668 (1933).

———, "Constitution and Court as Symbols," 46 *Yale L. J.* 1290 (1937).

———, "Appeals From the Supreme Court," 144 *Nation* 187 (1937).

Levy, Beryl H. *Our Constitution: Tool or Testament?.* New York: Alfred A. Knopf, Inc., 1941.

Lewinson, Joseph L. *Limiting Judicial Review.* Los Angeles: Parker, Stone & Baird Co., 1937.

Lippmann, Walter. *The Supreme Court: Independent or Controlled?.* New York: Harper & Brothers, 1937.

Loftin, S. M., "Independence of the Judiciary," 21 *A.B.A.J.* 469 (1935).

Manion, Clarence E., "Reviewing Judicial Review," 12 *Ind. L. J.* 167 (1937).

Mason, Alpheus T., "Politics and the Supreme Court," 85 *U. of Pa. L. Rev.* 659 (1937).

McBain, Howard Lee, "Some Proposals for Altering Judicial Review," 16 *B.U.L. Rev.* 874 (1936).

———, "Some Aspects of Judicial Review," 16 *B.U.L. Rev.* 525 (1936).

McCormac, E. I., "The Supreme Court and Unconstitutional Laws," 25 *Cal. L. Rev.* 552 (1937).

Merrill, M. H., "Judicial Supremacy in a Time of Change," 20 *Ia. L. Rev.* 594 (1935).

Meyer, E. F., "Debates of the Constitutional Convention on the Jurisdiction of the Supreme Court," 5 *Rocky Mt. L. Rev.* 168 (1933).

Murray, William H. *The President, the Supreme Court and Seven Senators.* Boston: Meador Publishing Company, 1939.

Newman, J. B., "Judicial Control Under the Federal Constitution," 14 *Tenn. L. Rev.* 1 (1935).

Nichols, Egbert R. *Congress or the Supreme Court: Which Shall Rule America?.* New York: Noble & Noble, Publishers, Inc., 1935.

Nilsson, G. W., "The Power of the Supreme Court to Declare Acts of Congress Unconstitutional," 12 *Cal. S.B.J.* 170 (1937).

O'Hara, Barratt, and Marie Crowe. *Who Made the Constitution? With the Authority for the Charge of Usurpation by the Judges.* Chicago: The Author, 1936.

Oxtoby, J. V., "Power of the Courts to Declare Acts of Congress Unconstitutional," 6 *Det. L. Rev.* 145 (1936).

Patterson, Caleb P., "James Madison and Judicial Review," 28 *Cal. L. Rev.* 22 (1939).

———, "The Development and Evaluation of Judicial Review," 13 *Wash. L. Rev.* 75, 171, 353 (1939).

Peake, James F., "Power of the Supreme Court to Nullify Acts of Congress," 8 *Const. Rev.* 83 (1934).

Pearson, Drew, and Robert Allen. *The Nine Old Men*. New York: Doubleday, Doran & Company, Inc., 1936.

———. *Nine Old Men at the Crossroads*. New York: Doubleday, Doran & Company, Inc., 1937.

Powell, Thomas Reed, "From Philadelphia to Philadelphia," 32 *Am. Pol. Sci. Rev.* 1 (1938).

———, "The Court, The Constitution and The Country," 16 *Sat. Rev. of Lit.* 3 (1937).

Pusey, Merlo. *The Supreme Court Crisis*. New York: The Macmillan Co., 1937.

Shea, F. M., "Consideration of Arguments for Judicial Review," 62 *N.Y.S. B.A.J.* 259 (1939).

Swaney, Charles B., "Congress and the Supreme Court," 12 *Soc. Sci.* 176 (1937).

Stone, I. F., (Isidor Feinstein). *The Court Disposes*. New York: Covici, Friede, Inc., 1937.

Tansill, Charles C., "The American Doctrine of Judicial Review," 2 *Vital Speeches* 597 (1936).

Thomas, Norman, "The Issue of the Constitution," 90 *New Rep.* 30 (1937).

Umbreit, K. C., "Tradition and Judicial Review," 26 *A.B.A.J.* 208 (1940).

White, T. R., "Disturbing the Balance," 85 *U. of Pa. L. Rev.* 678 (1937).

Wickersham, Cornelius W., Jr., "Consideration of Arguments Against Judicial Review," 62 *N.Y.S. B.A.J.* 266 (1939).

Worsoff, L. A., "The Judicial Veto," 27 *Ky. L. J.* 45 (1938).

Wright, Benjamin F. *American Interpretations of Natural Law*. Cambridge, Mass.: Harvard University Press, 1930.

Debate over the "New" Supreme Court, 1954-1961

Bickel, Alexander, "Court Curbing Time," 140 New Rep. 10 (1959).

Black, Charles L., Jr., *The People and the Court*. New York: The Macmillan Co., 1960.

Bloch, Charles. *States Rights: the Law of the Land*. Atlanta: The Harrison Company, 1958.

Brandwen, Maxwell, "The Supreme Court—Current Criticism in Perspective," *Nation* (1958).

Byrnes, James F., "The South Respects the Written Constitution," 23 *Vital Speeches* 331 (1957).

———, "The Supreme Court Must be Curbed," *U.S. News and World Report* (May 18, 1956), p. 50.

HISTORICAL BIBLIOGRAPHY

Call, Joseph L., "Judicial Review vs. Judicial Supremacy," 62 *Dick. L. Rev.* 71 (1957).

Cahn, Edmond, "Brief for the Supreme Court," *New York Times Magazine* (Oct. 7, 1956), p. 9.

Curtis, Charles P. *Law as Large as Life*. New York: Simon & Shuster, Inc., 1959.

Dahl, Robert A., "Decision-Making in a Democracy: The Role of the Supreme Court as a National Policy-Maker," 6 *J. of Pub. L.* 279 (1957).

Davis, Forrest, "The Court Reaches for Total Power," 4 *Nat. Rev.* 33 (1957).

Dean, H. E., "Judicial Review, Judicial Legislation, and Judicial Oligarchy," 34 *Ore. L. Rev.* 20 (1954).

Detmers, John R., "The Power of Judicial Restraint," 43 *Mass. L.Q.* 78 (1958).

Dunsford, John E., and Richard J. Childress, "Attacks on the Supreme Court," 7 *Soc. Order* 453 (1957).

Elliott, S. D., "Court-Curbing Proposals in Congress," 33 *Notre Dame* 597 (1958).

Ervin, Sam J., "The Role of the Supreme Court as the Interpreter of the Constitution," address printed in *Cong. Rec.*, Feb. 23, 1959, A 1305.

———, "The Power to Interpret is Not the Power to Amend," *U.S. News and World Report* (May 11, 1959), p. 120.

Fordham, Jefferson, "The Supreme Court: A Political Instrument," 24 *Vital Speeches* 650 (1958).

Frank, John P. *Marble Palace*. New York: Alfred A. Knopf, Inc., 1958.

Gordon, Rosalie. *Nine Men Against America*. New York: The Devin-Adair Company, Publishers, 1958.

Hand, Learned. *The Bill of Rights*. Cambridge, Mass.: Harvard University Press, 1958.

Hazlitt, Henry, "Court or Constitution? The Supreme Court's Steady Usurpation of Power," 2 *Nat. Rev.* 14 (1956).

Hennings, Thomas C., Jr., "The United States Supreme Court: The Ultimate Guardian of Our Freedom," 44 *A.B.A.J.* 213 (1958).

Jaffe, Louis L., "The Court Debated: Another View," *New York Times Magazine* (June 5, 1960), p. 36.

Kurland, Philip B., "The Supreme Court and its Judicial Critics," 6 *Utah L. Rev.* 457 (1959).

Lawrence, David, "What Written Constitution?" *U.S. News & World Report* (June 29, 1959), p. 104.

Long, Hamilton A. *Usurpers, Foes of Free Men*. New York: Post Printing Co., 1957.

Losos, J. O., "The Supreme Court and its Critics," 21 *Rev. of Pol.* 495 (1959).

Mason, Alpheus T., "The Supreme Court: Temple and Forum," 48 *Yale Rev.* 524 (1959).

———. *The Supreme Court from Taft to Warren*. Baton Rouge: Louisiana State University Press, 1958.

McGowan, Carl, "The Role of the Supreme Court in the American Constitutional System," 33 *Notre Dame Lawyer* 527 (1958).

McWhinney, Edward, "The Great Debate," 33 *N.Y.U. L. Rev.* 775 (1958).

Menez, Joseph F., "A Brief in Support of the Supreme Court," 54 *Northwestern U. L. Rev.* 30 (1959).

Nathanson, Nathaniel N., "The Supreme Court as a Unit of the National Government," 6 *J. of Pub. L.* 331 (1957).

Pittman, R. Carter, "The Supremacy of the Judiciary: A Study of Pre-constitutional History," 40 *A.B.A.J.* 389 (1954).

———, "The Law of the Land," 6 *J. of Pub. L.* 444 (1957).

Pollak, Louis, "The Supreme Court Under Fire," 6 *J. of Pub. L.* 428 (1957).

Pritchett, C. Herman. *The Political Offender and the Warren Court.* Boston: Boston University Press, 1958.

Rankin, J. Lee, "An Independent Supreme Court," 20 *U. of Pitt. L. Rev.* 785 (1959).

Rodell, Fred. *Nine Men.* New York: Random House, Inc., 1955.

———, "Crux of the Court Hullabaloo," *New York Times Magazine* (May 29, 1960), p. 13.

Rostow, Eugene V., "The Supreme Court and the People's Will," 33 *Notre Dame Lawyer* 573 (1958).

Schwartz, Bernard, "Is the Criticism of the High Court Valid?" *New York Times Magazine* (Aug. 25, 1957), p. 14.

Taylor, Telford, "Is the Supreme Court Supreme?" *New York Times Magazine* (Oct. 5, 1958), p. 10.

Vetter, George M., Jr., "Who is Supreme: People, Court or Legislature?" 45 *A.B.A.J.* 1051 (1959).

Wechsler, Herbert, "Toward Neutral Principles of Constitutional Law," 73 *Harv. L. Rev.* 1 (1959).

Weissman, D. L., "The Warren Court and its Critics," 23 *Prog.* 21 (1959).

Westin, Alan F., "Liberals and the Supreme Court: Making Peace With the 'Nine Old Men'," 22 *Commentary* 20 (1956).

———, "The Supreme Court Decisions: The New Balance on Civil Liberties," *New Leader* (Aug. 5, 1957), p. 5.

———, "The Supreme Court and Group Conflict," 52 *Am. Pol. Sci. Rev.* 665 (1958).

———, "When the Public Judges the Court," *New York Times Magazine* (May 31, 1958), p. 16.

A Selected Bibliography
of Public Comments
by Members of the Supreme Court
About the Power of Judicial Review, 1790-1961

The titles on this list were selected from the speeches and extra-judicial writings of the Justices after they joined the Court. These are representative samples of what the Justices have said in public about the Court's general powers of judicial review, their review of congressional legislation, and the basis of the Court's role as Constitutional umpire within the Federal Government. The dates beside each Justice's name are his years on the Court.

Baldwin, Henry (1830-1844)
  A General View of the Origin and Nature of the Constitution and Government of the United States. Philadelphia: John C. Clark, 1837.

Brennan, William J., Jr. (1956-   )
  "Remarks," *Student Legal Forum,* Charlottesville, Virginia, February 17, 1959.

Brewer, David J. (1890-1910)
  "The Nation's Safeguard," 16th Annual Meeting, *Proceedings of the N.Y. St. Bar Assoc.,* Jan. 17-18, 1893, p. 37.
  "The Federal Judiciary," 12th Ann. Meeting, *Bar Assoc. of St. of Kansas,* Jan. 16-17, 1895, p. 81.
  "The Nation's Anchor," 57 *Alb. L. J.* 166 (1898).
  "The Supreme Court of the United States," 33 *Scribner's* 273 (1903).
  "Two Periods in the History of the Supreme Court," 18th Annual Meeting, *Va. St. Bar Assoc.,* Aug. 7-9, 1906.

Brown, Henry Billings (1891-1906)
  "The Judiciary," in *Addresses on the Celebration of the 100th Anniversary of the Laying of the Cornerstone of the Capitol of the United States,* p. 74, ed. Duncan S. Walker. Washington, D.C.: 1896.

Burton, Harold H. (1945-1958)
  "The Cornerstone of American Constitutional Law: The Extraordinary Case of *Marbury v. Madison*," 36 *A.B.A.J.* 805 (1950).

147

Clark, Tom C. (1949-   )
"Constitutional Adjudication and the Supreme Court," 9 *Drake L. Rev.* 59 (1960).

Clarke, John H. (1916-1922)
"Judicial Power to Declare Legislation Unconstitutional," 9 *A.B.A.J.* 689 (1923).

Douglas, William O. (1939-   )
We The Judges: Studies in American and Indian Constitutional Law from Marshall to Mukherjea. New York: Doubleday & Co., Inc., 1956.
"Legal Institutions in America," Speech at the Centennial of Columbia U. Law School, New York, November 8, 1958.

Field, Stephen J. (1863-1899)
"The Supreme Court of the United States," Address at Centennial Celebration of the Organization of the Federal Judiciary, February 4, 1890, New York City, 134 U.S. 729 (1890).

Frankfurter, Felix (1939-   )
"Some Observations on Supreme Court Litigation and Legal Education," Law School, U. of Chicago, 1954.
"Some Observations on the Nature of the Judicial Process of Supreme Court Litigation," *Proceedings of the Am. Phil. Soc.,* Vol 98, No. 4, August, 1954.
"John Marshall and the Judicial Function," 69 *Harv. L. Rev.* 217 (1955).

Harlan, John Marshall (1877-1911)
"The Supreme Court of the United States," Centennial Celebration of the Organization of the Federal Judiciary, 134 U.S. 751 (1890).
"The Courts in the American System of Government," 37 *Chi. L. News* 271 (1905).
"Government Under the Constitution," *Il. Law Notes* 206, (1908).

Holmes, Oliver Wendell (1902-1932)
"John Marshall," in *The Mind and Faith of Justice Holmes,* p. 382, ed. Max Lerner. Boston: Little, Brown & Co., 1943.

Hughes, Charles Evans (1910-1916, 1930-1941)
The Supreme Court of the United States. New York: Columbia University Press, 1928.

Jackson, Robert H. (1941-1954)
The Supreme Court in the American System of Government. Cambridge, Mass.: Harvard University Press, 1955.

Lurton, Horace (1900-1914)
"A Government of Law or a Government of Men," 193 *North Am. Rev.* 9 (1911).

Matthews, Stanley (1881-1889)
"The Judicial Power of the United States," Address before the 64th Anniversary Celebration of Yale Law School, June 26, 1888, Yale Law Library.
"The Federal Judiciary" in *History of the Celebration of the One Hundredth Anniversary of the Promulgation of the Constitution of the United States,* II, 370, ed. Hampton Carson. Philadelphia: J. B. Lippincott Co.

BIBLIOGRAPHY OF PUBLIC COMMENTS

Miller, Samuel F. (1862-1890)

Lectures on the Constitution. Washington, D.C.: Morrison, 1880.

Addresses: The Constitution and the Supreme Court of the United States. New York: D. Appleton, 1889.

Lectures on the Constitution of the United States. New York: Banks, 1893.

Reed, Stanley (1938-1957)

"Our Constitutional Philosophy: Concerning the Significance of Judicial Review in the Evolution of American Democracy," Speech to Kentucky Bar Assoc., April 4, 1957.

Roberts, Owen D. (1930-1945)

"Now is the Time: Fortifying the Independence of the Supreme Court," 35 *A.B.A.J.* 1 (1949).

The Court and the Constitution. Cambridge, Mass.: Harvard University Press, 1951.

Stone, Harlan F. (1925-1941, 1941-1946)

"Fifty Years Work of the United States Supreme Court," 14 *A.B.A.J.* 428 (1929).

Story, Joseph (1811-1845)

Commentaries on the Constitution of the United States. Boston: Hilliard, Gray, 1833.

Sutherland, George (1922-1938)

Speech, *Proceedings of the 20th Annual Session of the State Bar Assoc. of Utah* (1924), pp. 55-67.

A CATALOG OF SELECTED
DOVER BOOKS
IN ALL FIELDS OF INTEREST

A CATALOG OF SELECTED DOVER
BOOKS IN ALL FIELDS OF INTEREST

CONCERNING THE SPIRITUAL IN ART, Wassily Kandinsky. Pioneering work by father of abstract art. Thoughts on color theory, nature of art. Analysis of earlier masters. 12 illustrations. 80pp. of text. 5⅜ x 8½.   23411-8

ANIMALS: 1,419 Copyright-Free Illustrations of Mammals, Birds, Fish, Insects, etc., Jim Harter (ed.). Clear wood engravings present, in extremely lifelike poses, over 1,000 species of animals. One of the most extensive pictorial sourcebooks of its kind. Captions. Index. 284pp. 9 x 12.   23766-4

CELTIC ART: The Methods of Construction, George Bain. Simple geometric techniques for making Celtic interlacements, spirals, Kells-type initials, animals, humans, etc. Over 500 illustrations. 160pp. 9 x 12. (Available in U.S. only.)   22923-8

AN ATLAS OF ANATOMY FOR ARTISTS, Fritz Schider. Most thorough reference work on art anatomy in the world. Hundreds of illustrations, including selections from works by Vesalius, Leonardo, Goya, Ingres, Michelangelo, others. 593 illustrations. 192pp. 7⅛ x 10¼.   20241-0

CELTIC HAND STROKE-BY-STROKE (Irish Half-Uncial from "The Book of Kells"): An Arthur Baker Calligraphy Manual, Arthur Baker. Complete guide to creating each letter of the alphabet in distinctive Celtic manner. Covers hand position, strokes, pens, inks, paper, more. Illustrated. 48pp. 8¼ x 11.   24336-2

EASY ORIGAMI, John Montroll. Charming collection of 32 projects (hat, cup, pelican, piano, swan, many more) specially designed for the novice origami hobbyist. Clearly illustrated easy-to-follow instructions insure that even beginning papercrafters will achieve successful results. 48pp. 8¼ x 11.   27298-2

THE COMPLETE BOOK OF BIRDHOUSE CONSTRUCTION FOR WOODWORKERS, Scott D. Campbell. Detailed instructions, illustrations, tables. Also data on bird habitat and instinct patterns. Bibliography. 3 tables. 63 illustrations in 15 figures. 48pp. 5¼ x 8½.   24407-5

BLOOMINGDALE'S ILLUSTRATED 1886 CATALOG: Fashions, Dry Goods and Housewares, Bloomingdale Brothers. Famed merchants' extremely rare catalog depicting about 1,700 products: clothing, housewares, firearms, dry goods, jewelry, more. Invaluable for dating, identifying vintage items. Also, copyright-free graphics for artists, designers. Co-published with Henry Ford Museum & Greenfield Village. 160pp. 8¼ x 11.   25780-0

HISTORIC COSTUME IN PICTURES, Braun & Schneider. Over 1,450 costumed figures in clearly detailed engravings–from dawn of civilization to end of 19th century. Captions. Many folk costumes. 256pp. 8⅜ x 11¾.   23150-X

STICKLEY CRAFTSMAN FURNITURE CATALOGS, Gustav Stickley and L. & J. G. Stickley. Beautiful, functional furniture in two authentic catalogs from 1910. 594 illustrations, including 277 photos, show settles, rockers, armchairs, reclining chairs, bookcases, desks, tables. 183pp. 6½ x 9¼.   23838-5

AMERICAN LOCOMOTIVES IN HISTORIC PHOTOGRAPHS: 1858 to 1949, Ron Ziel (ed.). A rare collection of 126 meticulously detailed official photographs, called "builder portraits," of American locomotives that majestically chronicle the rise of steam locomotive power in America. Introduction. Detailed captions. xi+ 129pp. 9 x 12.   27393-8

AMERICA'S LIGHTHOUSES: An Illustrated History, Francis Ross Holland, Jr. Delightfully written, profusely illustrated fact-filled survey of over 200 American lighthouses since 1716. History, anecdotes, technological advances, more. 240pp. 8 x 10¾.
                                        25576-X

TOWARDS A NEW ARCHITECTURE, Le Corbusier. Pioneering manifesto by founder of "International School." Technical and aesthetic theories, views of industry, economics, relation of form to function, "mass-production split" and much more. Profusely illustrated. 320pp. 6⅛ x 9¼. (Available in U.S. only.)   25023-7

HOW THE OTHER HALF LIVES, Jacob Riis. Famous journalistic record, exposing poverty and degradation of New York slums around 1900, by major social reformer. 100 striking and influential photographs. 233pp. 10 x 7⅞.   22012-5

FRUIT KEY AND TWIG KEY TO TREES AND SHRUBS, William M. Harlow. One of the handiest and most widely used identification aids. Fruit key covers 120 deciduous and evergreen species; twig key 160 deciduous species. Easily used. Over 300 photographs. 126pp. 5⅜ x 8½.   20511-8

COMMON BIRD SONGS, Dr. Donald J. Borror. Songs of 60 most common U.S. birds: robins, sparrows, cardinals, bluejays, finches, more—arranged in order of increasing complexity. Up to 9 variations of songs of each species.
                                        Cassette and manual 99911-4

ORCHIDS AS HOUSE PLANTS, Rebecca Tyson Northen. Grow cattleyas and many other kinds of orchids—in a window, in a case, or under artificial light. 63 illustrations. 148pp. 5⅜ x 8½.   23261-1

MONSTER MAZES, Dave Phillips. Masterful mazes at four levels of difficulty. Avoid deadly perils and evil creatures to find magical treasures. Solutions for all 32 exciting illustrated puzzles. 48pp. 8¼ x 11.   26005-4

MOZART'S DON GIOVANNI (DOVER OPERA LIBRETTO SERIES), Wolfgang Amadeus Mozart. Introduced and translated by Ellen H. Bleiler. Standard Italian libretto, with complete English translation. Convenient and thoroughly portable—an ideal companion for reading along with a recording or the performance itself. Introduction. List of characters. Plot summary. 121pp. 5¼ x 8½.   24944-1

TECHNICAL MANUAL AND DICTIONARY OF CLASSICAL BALLET, Gail Grant. Defines, explains, comments on steps, movements, poses and concepts. 15-page pictorial section. Basic book for student, viewer. 127pp. 5⅜ x 8½.   21843-0

THE CLARINET AND CLARINET PLAYING, David Pino. Lively, comprehensive work features suggestions about technique, musicianship, and musical interpretation, as well as guidelines for teaching, making your own reeds, and preparing for public performance. Includes an intriguing look at clarinet history. "A godsend," *The Clarinet,* Journal of the International Clarinet Society. Appendixes. 7 illus. 320pp. 5⅜ x 8½. 40270-3

HOLLYWOOD GLAMOR PORTRAITS, John Kobal (ed.). 145 photos from 1926-49. Harlow, Gable, Bogart, Bacall; 94 stars in all. Full background on photographers, technical aspects. 160pp. 8⅜ x 11¼. 23352-9

THE ANNOTATED CASEY AT THE BAT: A Collection of Ballads about the Mighty Casey/Third, Revised Edition, Martin Gardner (ed.). Amusing sequels and parodies of one of America's best-loved poems: Casey's Revenge, Why Casey Whiffed, Casey's Sister at the Bat, others. 256pp. 5⅜ x 8½. 28598-7

THE RAVEN AND OTHER FAVORITE POEMS, Edgar Allan Poe. Over 40 of the author's most memorable poems: "The Bells," "Ulalume," "Israfel," "To Helen," "The Conqueror Worm," "Eldorado," "Annabel Lee," many more. Alphabetic lists of titles and first lines. 64pp. 5³⁄₁₆ x 8¼. 26685-0

PERSONAL MEMOIRS OF U. S. GRANT, Ulysses Simpson Grant. Intelligent, deeply moving firsthand account of Civil War campaigns, considered by many the finest military memoirs ever written. Includes letters, historic photographs, maps and more. 528pp. 6⅛ x 9¼. 28587-1

ANCIENT EGYPTIAN MATERIALS AND INDUSTRIES, A. Lucas and J. Harris. Fascinating, comprehensive, thoroughly documented text describes this ancient civilization's vast resources and the processes that incorporated them in daily life, including the use of animal products, building materials, cosmetics, perfumes and incense, fibers, glazed ware, glass and its manufacture, materials used in the mummification process, and much more. 544pp. 6⅛ x 9¼. (Available in U.S. only.) 40446-3

RUSSIAN STORIES/RUSSKIE RASSKAZY: A Dual-Language Book, edited by Gleb Struve. Twelve tales by such masters as Chekhov, Tolstoy, Dostoevsky, Pushkin, others. Excellent word-for-word English translations on facing pages, plus teaching and study aids, Russian/English vocabulary, biographical/critical introductions, more. 416pp. 5⅜ x 8½. 26244-8

PHILADELPHIA THEN AND NOW: 60 Sites Photographed in the Past and Present, Kenneth Finkel and Susan Oyama. Rare photographs of City Hall, Logan Square, Independence Hall, Betsy Ross House, other landmarks juxtaposed with contemporary views. Captures changing face of historic city. Introduction. Captions. 128pp. 8¼ x 11. 25790-8

AIA ARCHITECTURAL GUIDE TO NASSAU AND SUFFOLK COUNTIES, LONG ISLAND, The American Institute of Architects, Long Island Chapter, and the Society for the Preservation of Long Island Antiquities. Comprehensive, well-researched and generously illustrated volume brings to life over three centuries of Long Island's great architectural heritage. More than 240 photographs with authoritative, extensively detailed captions. 176pp. 8¼ x 11. 26946-9

NORTH AMERICAN INDIAN LIFE: Customs and Traditions of 23 Tribes, Elsie Clews Parsons (ed.). 27 fictionalized essays by noted anthropologists examine religion, customs, government, additional facets of life among the Winnebago, Crow, Zuni, Eskimo, other tribes. 480pp. 6⅛ x 9¼. 27377-6

FRANK LLOYD WRIGHT'S DANA HOUSE, Donald Hoffmann. Pictorial essay of residential masterpiece with over 160 interior and exterior photos, plans, elevations, sketches and studies. 128pp. 9¼ x 10¾.   29120-0

THE MALE AND FEMALE FIGURE IN MOTION: 60 Classic Photographic Sequences, Eadweard Muybridge. 60 true-action photographs of men and women walking, running, climbing, bending, turning, etc., reproduced from rare 19th-century masterpiece. vi + 121pp. 9 x 12.   24745-7

1001 QUESTIONS ANSWERED ABOUT THE SEASHORE, N. J. Berrill and Jacquelyn Berrill. Queries answered about dolphins, sea snails, sponges, starfish, fishes, shore birds, many others. Covers appearance, breeding, growth, feeding, much more. 305pp. 5¼ x 8¼.   23366-9

ATTRACTING BIRDS TO YOUR YARD, William J. Weber. Easy-to-follow guide offers advice on how to attract the greatest diversity of birds: birdhouses, feeders, water and waterers, much more. 96pp. 5³⁄₁₆ x 8¼.   28927-3

MEDICINAL AND OTHER USES OF NORTH AMERICAN PLANTS: A Historical Survey with Special Reference to the Eastern Indian Tribes, Charlotte Erichsen-Brown. Chronological historical citations document 500 years of usage of plants, trees, shrubs native to eastern Canada, northeastern U.S. Also complete identifying information. 343 illustrations. 544pp. 6½ x 9¼.   25951-X

STORYBOOK MAZES, Dave Phillips. 23 stories and mazes on two-page spreads: Wizard of Oz, Treasure Island, Robin Hood, etc. Solutions. 64pp. 8¼ x 11.   23628-5

AMERICAN NEGRO SONGS: 230 Folk Songs and Spirituals, Religious and Secular, John W. Work. This authoritative study traces the African influences of songs sung and played by black Americans at work, in church, and as entertainment. The author discusses the lyric significance of such songs as "Swing Low, Sweet Chariot," "John Henry," and others and offers the words and music for 230 songs. Bibliography. Index of Song Titles. 272pp. 6½ x 9¼.   40271-1

MOVIE-STAR PORTRAITS OF THE FORTIES, John Kobal (ed.). 163 glamor, studio photos of 106 stars of the 1940s: Rita Hayworth, Ava Gardner, Marlon Brando, Clark Gable, many more. 176pp. 8⅜ x 11¼.   23546-7

BENCHLEY LOST AND FOUND, Robert Benchley. Finest humor from early 30s, about pet peeves, child psychologists, post office and others. Mostly unavailable elsewhere. 73 illustrations by Peter Arno and others. 183pp. 5⅜ x 8½.   22410-4

YEKL and THE IMPORTED BRIDEGROOM AND OTHER STORIES OF YIDDISH NEW YORK, Abraham Cahan. Film Hester Street based on *Yekl* (1896). Novel, other stories among first about Jewish immigrants on N.Y.'s East Side. 240pp. 5⅜ x 8½.   22427-9

SELECTED POEMS, Walt Whitman. Generous sampling from *Leaves of Grass*. Twenty-four poems include "I Hear America Singing," "Song of the Open Road," "I Sing the Body Electric," "When Lilacs Last in the Dooryard Bloom'd," "O Captain! My Captain!"–all reprinted from an authoritative edition. Lists of titles and first lines. 128pp. 5³⁄₁₆ x 8¼.   26878-0

THE BEST TALES OF HOFFMANN, E. T. A. Hoffmann. 10 of Hoffmann's most important stories: "Nutcracker and the King of Mice," "The Golden Flowerpot," etc. 458pp. 5⅜ x 8½. 21793-0

FROM FETISH TO GOD IN ANCIENT EGYPT, E. A. Wallis Budge. Rich detailed survey of Egyptian conception of "God" and gods, magic, cult of animals, Osiris, more. Also, superb English translations of hymns and legends. 240 illustrations. 545pp. 5⅜ x 8½. 25803-3

FRENCH STORIES/CONTES FRANÇAIS: A Dual-Language Book, Wallace Fowlie. Ten stories by French masters, Voltaire to Camus: "Micromegas" by Voltaire; "The Atheist's Mass" by Balzac; "Minuet" by de Maupassant; "The Guest" by Camus, six more. Excellent English translations on facing pages. Also French-English vocabulary list, exercises, more. 352pp. 5⅜ x 8½. 26443-2

CHICAGO AT THE TURN OF THE CENTURY IN PHOTOGRAPHS: 122 Historic Views from the Collections of the Chicago Historical Society, Larry A. Viskochil. Rare large-format prints offer detailed views of City Hall, State Street, the Loop, Hull House, Union Station, many other landmarks, circa 1904-1913. Introduction. Captions. Maps. 144pp. 9⅜ x 12¼. 24656-6

OLD BROOKLYN IN EARLY PHOTOGRAPHS, 1865-1929, William Lee Younger. Luna Park, Gravesend race track, construction of Grand Army Plaza, moving of Hotel Brighton, etc. 157 previously unpublished photographs. 165pp. 8⅞ x 11¾. 23587-4

THE MYTHS OF THE NORTH AMERICAN INDIANS, Lewis Spence. Rich anthology of the myths and legends of the Algonquins, Iroquois, Pawnees and Sioux, prefaced by an extensive historical and ethnological commentary. 36 illustrations. 480pp. 5⅜ x 8½. 25967-6

AN ENCYCLOPEDIA OF BATTLES: Accounts of Over 1,560 Battles from 1479 B.C. to the Present, David Eggenberger. Essential details of every major battle in recorded history from the first battle of Megiddo in 1479 B.C. to Grenada in 1984. List of Battle Maps. New Appendix covering the years 1967-1984. Index. 99 illustrations. 544pp. 6½ x 9¼. 24913-1

SAILING ALONE AROUND THE WORLD, Captain Joshua Slocum. First man to sail around the world, alone, in small boat. One of great feats of seamanship told in delightful manner. 67 illustrations. 294pp. 5⅜ x 8½. 20326-3

ANARCHISM AND OTHER ESSAYS, Emma Goldman. Powerful, penetrating, prophetic essays on direct action, role of minorities, prison reform, puritan hypocrisy, violence, etc. 271pp. 5⅜ x 8½. 22484-8

MYTHS OF THE HINDUS AND BUDDHISTS, Ananda K. Coomaraswamy and Sister Nivedita. Great stories of the epics; deeds of Krishna, Shiva, taken from puranas, Vedas, folk tales; etc. 32 illustrations. 400pp. 5⅜ x 8½. 21759-0

THE TRAUMA OF BIRTH, Otto Rank. Rank's controversial thesis that anxiety neurosis is caused by profound psychological trauma which occurs at birth. 256pp. 5⅜ x 8½. 27974-X

A THEOLOGICO-POLITICAL TREATISE, Benedict Spinoza. Also contains unfinished Political Treatise. Great classic on religious liberty, theory of government on common consent. R. Elwes translation. Total of 421pp. 5⅜ x 8½. 20249-6

CATALOG OF DOVER BOOKS

MY BONDAGE AND MY FREEDOM, Frederick Douglass. Born a slave, Douglass became outspoken force in antislavery movement. The best of Douglass' autobiographies. Graphic description of slave life. 464pp. 5⅜ x 8½. 22457-0

FOLLOWING THE EQUATOR: A Journey Around the World, Mark Twain. Fascinating humorous account of 1897 voyage to Hawaii, Australia, India, New Zealand, etc. Ironic, bemused reports on peoples, customs, climate, flora and fauna, politics, much more. 197 illustrations. 720pp. 5⅜ x 8½. 26113-1

THE PEOPLE CALLED SHAKERS, Edward D. Andrews. Definitive study of Shakers: origins, beliefs, practices, dances, social organization, furniture and crafts, etc. 33 illustrations. 351pp. 5⅜ x 8½. 21081-2

THE MYTHS OF GREECE AND ROME, H. A. Guerber. A classic of mythology, generously illustrated, long prized for its simple, graphic, accurate retelling of the principal myths of Greece and Rome, and for its commentary on their origins and significance. With 64 illustrations by Michelangelo, Raphael, Titian, Rubens, Canova, Bernini and others. 480pp. 5⅜ x 8½. 27584-1

PSYCHOLOGY OF MUSIC, Carl E. Seashore. Classic work discusses music as a medium from psychological viewpoint. Clear treatment of physical acoustics, auditory apparatus, sound perception, development of musical skills, nature of musical feeling, host of other topics. 88 figures. 408pp. 5⅜ x 8½. 21851-1

THE PHILOSOPHY OF HISTORY, Georg W. Hegel. Great classic of Western thought develops concept that history is not chance but rational process, the evolution of freedom. 457pp. 5⅜ x 8½. 20112-0

THE BOOK OF TEA, Kakuzo Okakura. Minor classic of the Orient: entertaining, charming explanation, interpretation of traditional Japanese culture in terms of tea ceremony. 94pp. 5⅜ x 8½. 20070-1

LIFE IN ANCIENT EGYPT, Adolf Erman. Fullest, most thorough, detailed older account with much not in more recent books, domestic life, religion, magic, medicine, commerce, much more. Many illustrations reproduce tomb paintings, carvings, hieroglyphs, etc. 597pp. 5⅜ x 8½. 22632-8

SUNDIALS, Their Theory and Construction, Albert Waugh. Far and away the best, most thorough coverage of ideas, mathematics concerned, types, construction, adjusting anywhere. Simple, nontechnical treatment allows even children to build several of these dials. Over 100 illustrations. 230pp. 5⅜ x 8½. 22947-5

THEORETICAL HYDRODYNAMICS, L. M. Milne-Thomson. Classic exposition of the mathematical theory of fluid motion, applicable to both hydrodynamics and aerodynamics. Over 600 exercises. 768pp. 6⅛ x 9¼. 68970-0

SONGS OF EXPERIENCE: Facsimile Reproduction with 26 Plates in Full Color, William Blake. 26 full-color plates from a rare 1826 edition. Includes "The Tyger," "London," "Holy Thursday," and other poems. Printed text of poems. 48pp. 5¼ x 7. 24636-1

OLD-TIME VIGNETTES IN FULL COLOR, Carol Belanger Grafton (ed.). Over 390 charming, often sentimental illustrations, selected from archives of Victorian graphics—pretty women posing, children playing, food, flowers, kittens and puppies, smiling cherubs, birds and butterflies, much more. All copyright-free. 48pp. 9¼ x 12¼. 27269-9

PERSPECTIVE FOR ARTISTS, Rex Vicat Cole. Depth, perspective of sky and sea, shadows, much more, not usually covered. 391 diagrams, 81 reproductions of drawings and paintings. 279pp. 5⅜ x 8½. 22487-2

DRAWING THE LIVING FIGURE, Joseph Sheppard. Innovative approach to artistic anatomy focuses on specifics of surface anatomy, rather than muscles and bones. Over 170 drawings of live models in front, back and side views, and in widely varying poses. Accompanying diagrams. 177 illustrations. Introduction. Index. 144pp. 8⅜ x11¼. 26723-7

GOTHIC AND OLD ENGLISH ALPHABETS: 100 Complete Fonts, Dan X. Solo. Add power, elegance to posters, signs, other graphics with 100 stunning copyright-free alphabets: Blackstone, Dolbey, Germania, 97 more–including many lower-case, numerals, punctuation marks. 104pp. 8⅛ x 11. 24695-7

HOW TO DO BEADWORK, Mary White. Fundamental book on craft from simple projects to five-bead chains and woven works. 106 illustrations. 142pp. 5⅜ x 8. 20697-1

THE BOOK OF WOOD CARVING, Charles Marshall Sayers. Finest book for beginners discusses fundamentals and offers 34 designs. "Absolutely first rate . . . well thought out and well executed."–E. J. Tangerman. 118pp. 7¾ x 10⅝. 23654-4

ILLUSTRATED CATALOG OF CIVIL WAR MILITARY GOODS: Union Army Weapons, Insignia, Uniform Accessories, and Other Equipment, Schuyler, Hartley, and Graham. Rare, profusely illustrated 1846 catalog includes Union Army uniform and dress regulations, arms and ammunition, coats, insignia, flags, swords, rifles, etc. 226 illustrations. 160pp. 9 x 12. 24939-5

WOMEN'S FASHIONS OF THE EARLY 1900s: An Unabridged Republication of "New York Fashions, 1909," National Cloak & Suit Co. Rare catalog of mail-order fashions documents women's and children's clothing styles shortly after the turn of the century. Captions offer full descriptions, prices. Invaluable resource for fashion, costume historians. Approximately 725 illustrations. 128pp. 8⅜ x 11¼. 27276-1

THE 1912 AND 1915 GUSTAV STICKLEY FURNITURE CATALOGS, Gustav Stickley. With over 200 detailed illustrations and descriptions, these two catalogs are essential reading and reference materials and identification guides for Stickley furniture. Captions cite materials, dimensions and prices. 112pp. 6½ x 9¼. 26676-1

EARLY AMERICAN LOCOMOTIVES, John H. White, Jr. Finest locomotive engravings from early 19th century: historical (1804–74), main-line (after 1870), special, foreign, etc. 147 plates. 142pp. 11⅜ x 8¼. 22772-3

THE TALL SHIPS OF TODAY IN PHOTOGRAPHS, Frank O. Braynard. Lavishly illustrated tribute to nearly 100 majestic contemporary sailing vessels: Amerigo Vespucci, Clearwater, Constitution, Eagle, Mayflower, Sea Cloud, Victory, many more. Authoritative captions provide statistics, background on each ship. 190 black-and-white photographs and illustrations. Introduction. 128pp. 8⅞ x 11¾. 27163-3

LITTLE BOOK OF EARLY AMERICAN CRAFTS AND TRADES, Peter Stockham (ed.). 1807 children's book explains crafts and trades: baker, hatter, cooper, potter, and many others. 23 copperplate illustrations. 140pp. 4⅝ x 6. 23336-7

VICTORIAN FASHIONS AND COSTUMES FROM HARPER'S BAZAR, 1867–1898, Stella Blum (ed.). Day costumes, evening wear, sports clothes, shoes, hats, other accessories in over 1,000 detailed engravings. 320pp. 9⅜ x 12¼. 22990-4

GUSTAV STICKLEY, THE CRAFTSMAN, Mary Ann Smith. Superb study surveys broad scope of Stickley's achievement, especially in architecture. Design philosophy, rise and fall of the Craftsman empire, descriptions and floor plans for many Craftsman houses, more. 86 black-and-white halftones. 31 line illustrations. Introduction 208pp. 6½ x 9¼. 27210-9

THE LONG ISLAND RAIL ROAD IN EARLY PHOTOGRAPHS, Ron Ziel. Over 220 rare photos, informative text document origin (1844) and development of rail service on Long Island. Vintage views of early trains, locomotives, stations, passengers, crews, much more. Captions. 8⅞ x 11¾. 26301-0

VOYAGE OF THE LIBERDADE, Joshua Slocum. Great 19th-century mariner's thrilling, first-hand account of the wreck of his ship off South America, the 35-foot boat he built from the wreckage, and its remarkable voyage home. 128pp. 5⅜ x 8½. 40022-0

TEN BOOKS ON ARCHITECTURE, Vitruvius. The most important book ever written on architecture. Early Roman aesthetics, technology, classical orders, site selection, all other aspects. Morgan translation. 331pp. 5⅜ x 8½. 20645-9

THE HUMAN FIGURE IN MOTION, Eadweard Muybridge. More than 4,500 stopped-action photos, in action series, showing undraped men, women, children jumping, lying down, throwing, sitting, wrestling, carrying, etc. 390pp. 7⅞ x 10⅝. 20204-6 Clothbd.

TREES OF THE EASTERN AND CENTRAL UNITED STATES AND CANADA, William M. Harlow. Best one-volume guide to 140 trees. Full descriptions, woodlore, range, etc. Over 600 illustrations. Handy size. 288pp. 4½ x 6⅜. 20395-6

SONGS OF WESTERN BIRDS, Dr. Donald J. Borror. Complete song and call repertoire of 60 western species, including flycatchers, juncoes, cactus wrens, many more–includes fully illustrated booklet. Cassette and manual 99913-0

GROWING AND USING HERBS AND SPICES, Milo Miloradovich. Versatile handbook provides all the information needed for cultivation and use of all the herbs and spices available in North America. 4 illustrations. Index. Glossary. 236pp. 5⅜ x 8½. 25058-X

BIG BOOK OF MAZES AND LABYRINTHS, Walter Shepherd. 50 mazes and labyrinths in all–classical, solid, ripple, and more–in one great volume. Perfect inexpensive puzzler for clever youngsters. Full solutions. 112pp. 8⅛ x 11. 22951-3

PIANO TUNING, J. Cree Fischer. Clearest, best book for beginner, amateur. Simple repairs, raising dropped notes, tuning by easy method of flattened fifths. No previous skills needed. 4 illustrations. 201pp. 5⅜ x 8½.   23267-0

HINTS TO SINGERS, Lillian Nordica. Selecting the right teacher, developing confidence, overcoming stage fright, and many other important skills receive thoughtful discussion in this indispensible guide, written by a world-famous diva of four decades' experience. 96pp. 5⅜ x 8½.   40094-8

THE COMPLETE NONSENSE OF EDWARD LEAR, Edward Lear. All nonsense limericks, zany alphabets, Owl and Pussycat, songs, nonsense botany, etc., illustrated by Lear. Total of 320pp. 5⅜ x 8½. (Available in U.S. only.)   20167-8

VICTORIAN PARLOUR POETRY: An Annotated Anthology, Michael R. Turner. 117 gems by Longfellow, Tennyson, Browning, many lesser-known poets. "The Village Blacksmith," "Curfew Must Not Ring Tonight," "Only a Baby Small," dozens more, often difficult to find elsewhere. Index of poets, titles, first lines. xxiii + 325pp. 5⅜ x 8¼.   27044-0

DUBLINERS, James Joyce. Fifteen stories offer vivid, tightly focused observations of the lives of Dublin's poorer classes. At least one, "The Dead," is considered a masterpiece. Reprinted complete and unabridged from standard edition. 160pp. 5³⁄₁₆ x 8¼.   26870-5

GREAT WEIRD TALES: 14 Stories by Lovecraft, Blackwood, Machen and Others, S. T. Joshi (ed.). 14 spellbinding tales, including "The Sin Eater," by Fiona McLeod, "The Eye Above the Mantel," by Frank Belknap Long, as well as renowned works by R. H. Barlow, Lord Dunsany, Arthur Machen, W. C. Morrow and eight other masters of the genre. 256pp. 5⅜ x 8½. (Available in U.S. only.)   40436-6

THE BOOK OF THE SACRED MAGIC OF ABRAMELIN THE MAGE, translated by S. MacGregor Mathers. Medieval manuscript of ceremonial magic. Basic document in Aleister Crowley, Golden Dawn groups. 268pp. 5⅜ x 8½.   23211-5

NEW RUSSIAN-ENGLISH AND ENGLISH-RUSSIAN DICTIONARY, M. A. O'Brien. This is a remarkably handy Russian dictionary, containing a surprising amount of information, including over 70,000 entries. 366pp. 4½ x 6⅛.   20208-9

HISTORIC HOMES OF THE AMERICAN PRESIDENTS, Second, Revised Edition, Irvin Haas. A traveler's guide to American Presidential homes, most open to the public, depicting and describing homes occupied by every American President from George Washington to George Bush. With visiting hours, admission charges, travel routes. 175 photographs. Index. 160pp. 8¼ x 11.   26751-2

NEW YORK IN THE FORTIES, Andreas Feininger. 162 brilliant photographs by the well-known photographer, formerly with *Life* magazine. Commuters, shoppers, Times Square at night, much else from city at its peak. Captions by John von Hartz. 181pp. 9¼ x 10¾.   23585-8

INDIAN SIGN LANGUAGE, William Tomkins. Over 525 signs developed by Sioux and other tribes. Written instructions and diagrams. Also 290 pictographs. 111pp. 6⅛ x 9¼.   22029-X

CATALOG OF DOVER BOOKS

ANATOMY: A Complete Guide for Artists, Joseph Sheppard. A master of figure drawing shows artists how to render human anatomy convincingly. Over 460 illustrations. 224pp. 8⅜ x 11¼. 27279-6

MEDIEVAL CALLIGRAPHY: Its History and Technique, Marc Drogin. Spirited history, comprehensive instruction manual covers 13 styles (ca. 4th century through 15th). Excellent photographs; directions for duplicating medieval techniques with modern tools. 224pp. 8⅜ x 11¼. 26142-5

DRIED FLOWERS: How to Prepare Them, Sarah Whitlock and Martha Rankin. Complete instructions on how to use silica gel, meal and borax, perlite aggregate, sand and borax, glycerine and water to create attractive permanent flower arrangements. 12 illustrations. 32pp. 5⅜ x 8½. 21802-3

EASY-TO-MAKE BIRD FEEDERS FOR WOODWORKERS, Scott D. Campbell. Detailed, simple-to-use guide for designing, constructing, caring for and using feeders. Text, illustrations for 12 classic and contemporary designs. 96pp. 5⅜ x 8½. 25847-5

SCOTTISH WONDER TALES FROM MYTH AND LEGEND, Donald A. Mackenzie. 16 lively tales tell of giants rumbling down mountainsides, of a magic wand that turns stone pillars into warriors, of gods and goddesses, evil hags, powerful forces and more. 240pp. 5⅜ x 8½. 29677-6

THE HISTORY OF UNDERCLOTHES, C. Willett Cunnington and Phyllis Cunnington. Fascinating, well-documented survey covering six centuries of English undergarments, enhanced with over 100 illustrations: 12th-century laced-up bodice, footed long drawers (1795), 19th-century bustles, l9th-century corsets for men, Victorian "bust improvers," much more. 272pp. 5⅜ x 8¼. 27124-2

ARTS AND CRAFTS FURNITURE: The Complete Brooks Catalog of 1912, Brooks Manufacturing Co. Photos and detailed descriptions of more than 150 now very collectible furniture designs from the Arts and Crafts movement depict davenports, settees, buffets, desks, tables, chairs, bedsteads, dressers and more, all built of solid, quarter-sawed oak. Invaluable for students and enthusiasts of antiques, Americana and the decorative arts. 80pp. 6½ x 9¼. 27471-3

WILBUR AND ORVILLE: A Biography of the Wright Brothers, Fred Howard. Definitive, crisply written study tells the full story of the brothers' lives and work. A vividly written biography, unparalleled in scope and color, that also captures the spirit of an extraordinary era. 560pp. 6⅛ x 9¼. 40297-5

THE ARTS OF THE SAILOR: Knotting, Splicing and Ropework, Hervey Garrett Smith. Indispensable shipboard reference covers tools, basic knots and useful hitches; handsewing and canvas work, more. Over 100 illustrations. Delightful reading for sea lovers. 256pp. 5⅜ x 8½. 26440-8

FRANK LLOYD WRIGHT'S FALLINGWATER: The House and Its History, Second, Revised Edition, Donald Hoffmann. A total revision–both in text and illustrations–of the standard document on Fallingwater, the boldest, most personal architectural statement of Wright's mature years, updated with valuable new material from the recently opened Frank Lloyd Wright Archives. "Fascinating"–*The New York Times*. 116 illustrations. 128pp. 9¼ x 10¾. 27430-6

PHOTOGRAPHIC SKETCHBOOK OF THE CIVIL WAR, Alexander Gardner. 100 photos taken on field during the Civil War. Famous shots of Manassas Harper's Ferry, Lincoln, Richmond, slave pens, etc. 244pp. 10⅝ x 8¼. 22731-6

FIVE ACRES AND INDEPENDENCE, Maurice G. Kains. Great back-to-the-land classic explains basics of self-sufficient farming. The one book to get. 95 illustrations. 397pp. 5⅜ x 8½. 20974-1

SONGS OF EASTERN BIRDS, Dr. Donald J. Borror. Songs and calls of 60 species most common to eastern U.S.: warblers, woodpeckers, flycatchers, thrushes, larks, many more in high-quality recording. Cassette and manual 99912-2

A MODERN HERBAL, Margaret Grieve. Much the fullest, most exact, most useful compilation of herbal material. Gigantic alphabetical encyclopedia, from aconite to zedoary, gives botanical information, medical properties, folklore, economic uses, much else. Indispensable to serious reader. 161 illustrations. 888pp. 6½ x 9¼. 2-vol. set. (Available in U.S. only.) Vol. I: 22798-7
Vol. II: 22799-5

HIDDEN TREASURE MAZE BOOK, Dave Phillips. Solve 34 challenging mazes accompanied by heroic tales of adventure. Evil dragons, people-eating plants, blood-thirsty giants, many more dangerous adversaries lurk at every twist and turn. 34 mazes, stories, solutions. 48pp. 8¼ x 11. 24566-7

LETTERS OF W. A. MOZART, Wolfgang A. Mozart. Remarkable letters show bawdy wit, humor, imagination, musical insights, contemporary musical world; includes some letters from Leopold Mozart. 276pp. 5⅜ x 8½. 22859-2

BASIC PRINCIPLES OF CLASSICAL BALLET, Agrippina Vaganova. Great Russian theoretician, teacher explains methods for teaching classical ballet. 118 illustrations. 175pp. 5⅜ x 8½. 22036-2

THE JUMPING FROG, Mark Twain. Revenge edition. The original story of The Celebrated Jumping Frog of Calaveras County, a hapless French translation, and Twain's hilarious "retranslation" from the French. 12 illustrations. 66pp. 5⅜ x 8½. 22686-7

BEST REMEMBERED POEMS, Martin Gardner (ed.). The 126 poems in this superb collection of 19th- and 20th-century British and American verse range from Shelley's "To a Skylark" to the impassioned "Renascence" of Edna St. Vincent Millay and to Edward Lear's whimsical "The Owl and the Pussycat." 224pp. 5⅜ x 8½. 27165-X

COMPLETE SONNETS, William Shakespeare. Over 150 exquisite poems deal with love, friendship, the tyranny of time, beauty's evanescence, death and other themes in language of remarkable power, precision and beauty. Glossary of archaic terms. 80pp. 5³⁄₁₆ x 8¼. 26686-9

THE BATTLES THAT CHANGED HISTORY, Fletcher Pratt. Eminent historian profiles 16 crucial conflicts, ancient to modern, that changed the course of civilization. 352pp. 5⅜ x 8½. 41129-X

CATALOG OF DOVER BOOKS

THE WIT AND HUMOR OF OSCAR WILDE, Alvin Redman (ed.). More than 1,000 ripostes, paradoxes, wisecracks: Work is the curse of the drinking classes; I can resist everything except temptation; etc. 258pp. 5⅜ x 8½. 20602-5

SHAKESPEARE LEXICON AND QUOTATION DICTIONARY, Alexander Schmidt. Full definitions, locations, shades of meaning in every word in plays and poems. More than 50,000 exact quotations. 1,485pp. 6½ x 9¼. 2-vol. set.
Vol. 1: 22726-X
Vol. 2: 22727-8

SELECTED POEMS, Emily Dickinson. Over 100 best-known, best-loved poems by one of America's foremost poets, reprinted from authoritative early editions. No comparable edition at this price. Index of first lines. 64pp. 5³⁄₁₆ x 8¼. 26466-1

THE INSIDIOUS DR. FU-MANCHU, Sax Rohmer. The first of the popular mystery series introduces a pair of English detectives to their archnemesis, the diabolical Dr. Fu-Manchu. Flavorful atmosphere, fast-paced action, and colorful characters enliven this classic of the genre. 208pp. 5³⁄₁₆ x 8¼. 29898-1

THE MALLEUS MALEFICARUM OF KRAMER AND SPRENGER, translated by Montague Summers. Full text of most important witchhunter's "bible," used by both Catholics and Protestants. 278pp. 6⅝ x 10. 22802-9

SPANISH STORIES/CUENTOS ESPAÑOLES: A Dual-Language Book, Angel Flores (ed.). Unique format offers 13 great stories in Spanish by Cervantes, Borges, others. Faithful English translations on facing pages. 352pp. 5⅜ x 8½. 25399-6

GARDEN CITY, LONG ISLAND, IN EARLY PHOTOGRAPHS, 1869–1919, Mildred H. Smith. Handsome treasury of 118 vintage pictures, accompanied by carefully researched captions, document the Garden City Hotel fire (1899), the Vanderbilt Cup Race (1908), the first airmail flight departing from the Nassau Boulevard Aerodrome (1911), and much more. 96pp. 8⅞ x 11¾. 40669-5

OLD QUEENS, N.Y., IN EARLY PHOTOGRAPHS, Vincent F. Seyfried and William Asadorian. Over 160 rare photographs of Maspeth, Jamaica, Jackson Heights, and other areas. Vintage views of DeWitt Clinton mansion, 1939 World's Fair and more. Captions. 192pp. 8⅞ x 11. 26358-4

CAPTURED BY THE INDIANS: 15 Firsthand Accounts, 1750-1870, Frederick Drimmer. Astounding true historical accounts of grisly torture, bloody conflicts, relentless pursuits, miraculous escapes and more, by people who lived to tell the tale. 384pp. 5⅜ x 8½. 24901-8

THE WORLD'S GREAT SPEECHES (Fourth Enlarged Edition), Lewis Copeland, Lawrence W. Lamm, and Stephen J. McKenna. Nearly 300 speeches provide public speakers with a wealth of updated quotes and inspiration–from Pericles' funeral oration and William Jennings Bryan's "Cross of Gold Speech" to Malcolm X's powerful words on the Black Revolution and Earl of Spenser's tribute to his sister, Diana, Princess of Wales. 944pp. 5⅜ x 8⅜. 40903-1

THE BOOK OF THE SWORD, Sir Richard F. Burton. Great Victorian scholar/adventurer's eloquent, erudite history of the "queen of weapons"–from prehistory to early Roman Empire. Evolution and development of early swords, variations (sabre, broadsword, cutlass, scimitar, etc.), much more. 336pp. 6⅛ x 9¼. 25434-8

AUTOBIOGRAPHY: The Story of My Experiments with Truth, Mohandas K. Gandhi. Boyhood, legal studies, purification, the growth of the Satyagraha (nonviolent protest) movement. Critical, inspiring work of the man responsible for the freedom of India. 480pp. 5⅜ x 8½. (Available in U.S. only.) 24593-4

CELTIC MYTHS AND LEGENDS, T. W. Rolleston. Masterful retelling of Irish and Welsh stories and tales. Cuchulain, King Arthur, Deirdre, the Grail, many more. First paperback edition. 58 full-page illustrations. 512pp. 5⅜ x 8½. 26507-2

THE PRINCIPLES OF PSYCHOLOGY, William James. Famous long course complete, unabridged. Stream of thought, time perception, memory, experimental methods; great work decades ahead of its time. 94 figures. 1,391pp. 5⅜ x 8½. 2-vol. set.
Vol. I: 20381-6 Vol. II: 20382-4

THE WORLD AS WILL AND REPRESENTATION, Arthur Schopenhauer. Definitive English translation of Schopenhauer's life work, correcting more than 1,000 errors, omissions in earlier translations. Translated by E. F. J. Payne. Total of 1,269pp. 5⅜ x 8½. 2-vol. set. Vol. 1: 21761-2 Vol. 2: 21762-0

MAGIC AND MYSTERY IN TIBET, Madame Alexandra David-Neel. Experiences among lamas, magicians, sages, sorcerers, Bonpa wizards. A true psychic discovery. 32 illustrations. 321pp. 5⅜ x 8½. (Available in U.S. only.) 22682-4

THE EGYPTIAN BOOK OF THE DEAD, E. A. Wallis Budge. Complete reproduction of Ani's papyrus, finest ever found. Full hieroglyphic text, interlinear transliteration, word-for-word translation, smooth translation. 533pp. 6½ x 9¼. 21866-X

MATHEMATICS FOR THE NONMATHEMATICIAN, Morris Kline. Detailed, college-level treatment of mathematics in cultural and historical context, with numerous exercises. Recommended Reading Lists. Tables. Numerous figures. 641pp. 5⅜ x 8½.
24823-2

PROBABILISTIC METHODS IN THE THEORY OF STRUCTURES, Isaac Elishakoff. Well-written introduction covers the elements of the theory of probability from two or more random variables, the reliability of such multivariable structures, the theory of random function, Monte Carlo methods of treating problems incapable of exact solution, and more. Examples. 502pp. 5⅜ x 8½. 40691-1

THE RIME OF THE ANCIENT MARINER, Gustave Doré, S. T. Coleridge. Doré's finest work; 34 plates capture moods, subtleties of poem. Flawless full-size reproductions printed on facing pages with authoritative text of poem. "Beautiful. Simply beautiful."–*Publisher's Weekly.* 77pp. 9¼ x 12. 22305-1

NORTH AMERICAN INDIAN DESIGNS FOR ARTISTS AND CRAFTSPEOPLE, Eva Wilson. Over 360 authentic copyright-free designs adapted from Navajo blankets, Hopi pottery, Sioux buffalo hides, more. Geometrics, symbolic figures, plant and animal motifs, etc. 128pp. 8⅜ x 11. (Not for sale in the United Kingdom.) 25341-4

SCULPTURE: Principles and Practice, Louis Slobodkin. Step-by-step approach to clay, plaster, metals, stone; classical and modern. 253 drawings, photos. 255pp. 8⅛ x 11.
22960-2

THE INFLUENCE OF SEA POWER UPON HISTORY, 1660–1783, A. T. Mahan. Influential classic of naval history and tactics still used as text in war colleges. First paperback edition. 4 maps. 24 battle plans. 640pp. 5⅜ x 8½. 25509-3

CATALOG OF DOVER BOOKS

THE STORY OF THE TITANIC AS TOLD BY ITS SURVIVORS, Jack Winocour (ed.). What it was really like. Panic, despair, shocking inefficiency, and a little heroism. More thrilling than any fictional account. 26 illustrations. 320pp. 5⅜ x 8½.
20610-6

FAIRY AND FOLK TALES OF THE IRISH PEASANTRY, William Butler Yeats (ed.). Treasury of 64 tales from the twilight world of Celtic myth and legend: "The Soul Cages," "The Kildare Pooka," "King O'Toole and his Goose," many more. Introduction and Notes by W. B. Yeats. 352pp. 5⅜ x 8½.
26941-8

BUDDHIST MAHAYANA TEXTS, E. B. Cowell and others (eds.). Superb, accurate translations of basic documents in Mahayana Buddhism, highly important in history of religions. The Buddha-karita of Asvaghosha, Larger Sukhavativyuha, more. 448pp. 5⅜ x 8½.
25552-2

ONE TWO THREE . . . INFINITY: Facts and Speculations of Science, George Gamow. Great physicist's fascinating, readable overview of contemporary science: number theory, relativity, fourth dimension, entropy, genes, atomic structure, much more. 128 illustrations. Index. 352pp. 5⅜ x 8½.
25664-2

EXPERIMENTATION AND MEASUREMENT, W. J. Youden. Introductory manual explains laws of measurement in simple terms and offers tips for achieving accuracy and minimizing errors. Mathematics of measurement, use of instruments, experimenting with machines. 1994 edition. Foreword. Preface. Introduction. Epilogue. Selected Readings. Glossary. Index. Tables and figures. 128pp. 5⅜ x 8½.   40451-X

DALÍ ON MODERN ART: The Cuckolds of Antiquated Modern Art, Salvador Dalí. Influential painter skewers modern art and its practitioners. Outrageous evaluations of Picasso, Cézanne, Turner, more. 15 renderings of paintings discussed. 44 calligraphic decorations by Dalí. 96pp. 5⅜ x 8½. (Available in U.S. only.)
29220-7

ANTIQUE PLAYING CARDS: A Pictorial History, Henry René D'Allemagne. Over 900 elaborate, decorative images from rare playing cards (14th–20th centuries): Bacchus, death, dancing dogs, hunting scenes, royal coats of arms, players cheating, much more. 96pp. 9¼ x 12¼.
29265-7

MAKING FURNITURE MASTERPIECES: 30 Projects with Measured Drawings, Franklin H. Gottshall. Step-by-step instructions, illustrations for constructing handsome, useful pieces, among them a Sheraton desk, Chippendale chair, Spanish desk, Queen Anne table and a William and Mary dressing mirror. 224pp. 8⅛ x 11¼.
29338-6

THE FOSSIL BOOK: A Record of Prehistoric Life, Patricia V. Rich et al. Profusely illustrated definitive guide covers everything from single-celled organisms and dinosaurs to birds and mammals and the interplay between climate and man. Over 1,500 illustrations. 760pp. 7½ x 10⅛.
29371-8

Paperbound unless otherwise indicated. Available at your book dealer, online at **www.doverpublications.com**, or by writing to Dept. GI, Dover Publications, Inc., 31 East 2nd Street, Mineola, NY 11501. For current price information or for free catalogues (please indicate field of interest), write to Dover Publications or log on to **www.doverpublications.com** and see every Dover book in print. Dover publishes more than 500 books each year on science, elementary and advanced mathematics, biology, music, art, literary history, social sciences, and other areas.